A Kansan Conquers the Cosmos

or, "Spaced Out All My Life!"

ALAN GLINES

iUniverse, Inc.
New York   Bloomington

A Kansan Conquers the Cosmos
or, "Spaced Out All My Life!"

iUniverse books may be ordered through booksellers or by contacting:

iUniverse
1663 Liberty Drive
Bloomington, IN 47403
www.iuniverse.com
1-800-Authors (1-800-288-4677)

Because of the dynamic nature of the Internet, any Web addresses or links contained in this book may have changed since publication and may no longer be valid. The views expressed in this work are solely those of the author and do not necessarily reflect the views of the publisher, and the publisher hereby disclaims any responsibility for them.

ISBN: 978-1-4502-6441-9 (pbk)
ISBN: 978-1-4502-6443-3 (cloth)
ISBN: 978-1-4502-6442-6 (ebk)

Library of Congress Control Number: 2010938764

Printed in the United States of America

iUniverse rev. date: 11/16/10

Foreword

First of all, *A Kansan Conquers the Cosmos* is a wonderful read: It flows and is lots of fun; it captivated me and made me smile. The reader gets to love Alan both as the author and as the character in this touching autobiographical work, identifying with Alan as protagonist and becoming immersed in his narrative in ways reminiscent of the writings of Ernest K. Gann.

I have worked with Alan on and off for over forty years. We worked the 1973–1974 Skylab missions, he as Instrumentation and Communications Officer and I as Capsule Communicator. I flew my own six spaceflights but was also Capsule Communicator for twenty-five missions. Some of those were more challenging and rewarding than my six shuttle flights. I attained the same Mission Control spirit and dedication that Alan has lived for decades; that is, being on the playing field and being all you can be, all the time—living up to system and the Mission Control Center team expectations continuously.

Over four decades, Alan has acquired an extraordinarily rich tapestry of experience in the aerospace worlds of research and development, and command and control. He has a penetrating memory and comprehension for historical details, at times seemingly too detailed—but that is aerospace: The beauty is in the details, and if they are not dealt with, catastrophes can occur. In preparing to write this foreword, I read everything Alan sent to me with pleasure and enthusiasm both for the narrative and for the enlightenment of things I had not known before. It is a people book as well as a behind-the-scenes book.

This work feels similar to the bildungsroman genre of classical literature, wherein the principal themes are the physical, moral, and psychological growth of the individual. Alan follows the trajectory of a science-fiction child who ran a theater like a mission control and then went on to the actual NASA Mission Control and a myriad of disparate responsibilities, all of which reach back into his childhood dreams and endeavors. His life's dedication to the details inherent in systems operations makes his story seem almost predestined, just as the most likely reason that I was chosen to be the lead repairman-in-space of the Hubble Space Telescope is because I was first a farm kid then an aircraft mechanic in Korea with the Marine Corps. (See Chapter 9 for our mission together.)

Alan continuously enriches his main narrative with stories and anecdotes. His background in teaching and theater produces a sense of the dramatic, while his first-person, flowing stream of consciousness immerses you in the action.

I love this book and its autobiographical point of view. Alan is both a free spirit and a strict disciplinarian; he knew when to be creative and when to follow the rules, and so does the book. It is both creatively subjective and hard-fact objective, and the combination is magical. There are thousands of books about aerospace; this one is different. I look forward to reading it again.

Story Musgrave
NASA Astronaut

Chapter 1

Alan Meets His First Control Console: The KU Stage Lights

My affinity for control consoles, which eventually led me to Apollo Mission Control and my life's work in aerospace, began in 1959 at the University of Kansas (KU)—at the University Theatre, of all places. Control consoles are not like Captain Kirk's chair, where he commanded the *Enterprise* with voice callouts to his team. However, the other positions on the *Enterprise* had control consoles similar to mine at Apollo Mission Control.

A console can be as simple as a PC on a desk but is usually designed with more than one CRT (TV screen) and many indicator lights and push buttons that provide all the control, monitoring, and communications capability required by each position. One is connected to the console via headset and microphone, which frees one's hands to adjust video, press buttons, and select channels to communicate with colleagues.

Control consoles became a main theme early in my life, before I took over the ultimate control consoles at the "center of the universe." Starting in 1966, the center of the universe for much of my adult life was in Building 30, NASA Mission Control, at the brand-new Manned Spacecraft Center in Houston, Texas (later the Johnson Space Center). The three-story building looks like six with the addition of another five to ten feet of false floor and false ceiling space required for all the cabling in the building. More about this incredible place later.

The heart of the Mission Control Center (MCC) is the main control room comprised of approximately fifteen consoles (Figure 1). This is what's usually seen on television. We knew that room as the MOCR (pronounced "MOH-kerr"), which stands for Mission Operations Control Room. But I'm not there yet.

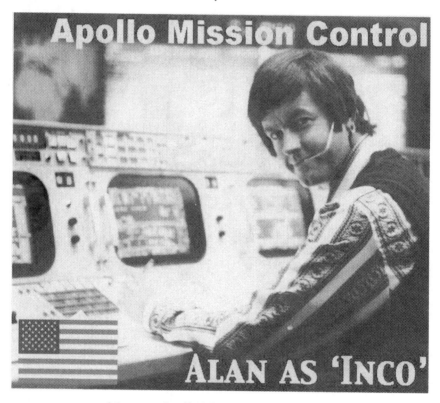

Me at my Apollo Mission Control console

In 1959, in a small room at the back of the brand-new University Theatre at the University of Kansas in Lawrence, I was a long way from Captain Kirk's *Enterprise* starship and many years from my console at the Apollo Mission Control Center in Houston (MCC-H). As a matter of fact, NASA's first Mission Control Center (MCC-K) had just been built for Alan Shepard's first flight into space in May 1961. It was located in a blockhouse near "missile row" on Cape Canaveral in Florida, adjacent to what is now called the Kennedy Space Center.

But in 1959 I was only sixteen years old, and I was drunk with power! There I was: a nerdy guy in total control of a major university summer production, manning the lighting console at the back of the balcony in the University Theatre. It was opening night of the play *The Member of the Wedding*. And thanks to Dr. Arthur Kean, the play's director, I was in charge of the house lights and all the stage lighting for the run of the play. I was well trained by Dr. Kean to perform the lighting cues on schedule throughout the opening and subsequent three weeks of performances. Captain Kirk would have been proud!

How did I get there in the summer of 1959? The story starts with my tenth-grade Speech class teacher, Mrs. McAlester. That class was the beginning of my long association with, and love of, live theater and show business. I was one of five lucky students selected for the Midwestern Music and Art Camp, a full summer of concentrated theater training at the University. There were only twenty-five of us under the concentrated care of the University Theatre faculty.

What an opportunity! I had no idea at the time, but I was smart enough to realize that it was a great adventure for this nerdy Kansan who had never been so far away from home on his own. I had journeyed to Kansas City once with my Little League baseball team to see Mickey Mantle, Roger Maris, Yogi Berra, and the rest of the Yankees play our Kansas City team, but that was it.

The full KU summer camp included our theater division along with other fine arts divisions, such as band, orchestra, chorus, ballet, and painting. The slang term for the long-running camp was "Band Camp." And it wasn't too much like a real camp; rather, we all stayed in modern university dormitory rooms. Everyone fit into the Carruth-O'Leary dormitory, I remember. It was within easy walking distance of all our theater locations.

More than six thousand high school students attended this camp. I had looked forward to meeting loads of people, but our theater schedule filled each day from morning to late evening. I met only a few people outside our group at the social events. Jeff (a colleague in the theater group at the camp) and I used to sneak over to the ballet division to watch all those beautiful girls dance in their tutus. (The second summer,

I fell in love with one. She was a small blonde lady from Oklahoma City named Cherri—my first true love. But I am getting ahead of myself!)

Our theater group came from high schools all over the state, Wichita and Kansas City, the larger metropolitan areas. With five of us from Independence, a town of ten thousand, we were somewhat over-represented. No matter. One or two camp members were from as far away as Des Moines, Iowa, and Oklahoma City, Oklahoma, as I recall.

Our normal day consisted of a heavy schedule from dawn to dark. In the morning we were scheduled in classes that included stagecraft for production. Afternoons were filled with a variety of backstage work, putting our morning classwork to use at the theater. We helped get a college production ready for performance, doing such tasks as scene building and cutting spotlight gels, and got training in makeup, sound and lights, and scene changing while at it.

The evenings were set aside for the rehearsals for our major production, *Once in a Lifetime*.

That's me on the far left, in the tux.

We were surprised to learn that we would be preparing and performing in a three-act musical production during our summer there. What a challenge for us "green" actors from high school! It made the intensity of our summer similar to traditional summer stock theater, and called for us to rise to the challenge, each with our own character and contribution to the show. The setting was the KU University Theatre with its new facilities and talented, capable faculty.

What I appreciated from the start was being treated as responsible college students instead of high school students. As a result, that is what we became: responsible. (Perhaps more so than we ever became!) Additionally, we had immediate responsibility for other acting roles in small one-act plays directed by the theater graduate students as part of our morning classes. And casting began immediately for all parts in Moss Hart's musical, *Once in a Lifetime*, directed by Dr. Jack Brookings. He had more confidence in us than we had in ourselves.

I knew nothing about that show and, thankfully, was cast in small parts where my singing, such as it was, was relegated to the background—nearly a non-singing part. (I was not a trained singer at all.) I say "thankfully" because that freed up more of my time for what was coming as the most important experience of the summer for this small-town nerd.

I first met Dr. Arthur Kean as a teacher of one of our morning classes in theater arts and crafts. I don't remember much about his class except it included a lot of stagecraft basics that were new to me. In getting to know his students, Dr. Kean had an ulterior motive. He needed staff for other work! He needed bodies for some of the backstage jobs on the college production because the usual availability of students was far less for the summer than the regular school year.

The brand-new University Theatre was a modern and well-equipped facility. For its main stage productions, it sparkled with the latest in high-tech lighting instruments. Technical control for all the lights and sound were optimally located in a soundproof booth at the rear of the balcony overlooking the audience and stage. In this room I met my first control console in the real world. Up to this point, science fiction novels had provided me with a wealth of imagined starship controls throughout the galaxy. Now I was about to venture into console control of my own starship called the KU University Theatre. "Beam me down, Scotty. This sixteen-year-old is ready to control from my first console!"

I lucked out. The technical director of the theater was my morning teacher, Dr. Arthur Kean. I guess from his perspective he lucked out, too. In his class he had a kid from Independence who was interested in more than just becoming a star actor. I loved the technical side of that new theater, something I had never seen before.

As I got to know Dr. Kean in class, he apparently saw my interest in the lighting side of the business. It wasn't long before he asked me if I wanted to help run the lights for the college production. He didn't have to ask me twice! He would be happy to teach me all I needed to learn about the console operation of complex matrix power-driven group master dimmers. I agreed without hesitation.

Now, understand that the incredible control that I would have every night of the production was not like the starships I had flown throughout the galaxy in my imagination. But the down-to-earth side of me knew that this was the reality I had prepared for all my life. And I loved it!

I was honored to be offered this responsibility and told Dr. Kean that I would work hard to assure a perfect production every night. However, some of the lighting tasks in the evening conflicted with rehearsals for our high school production. I lucked out again in that I had only a few small parts in *Once in a Lifetime*. This allowed me, with some innovative scheduling by Dr. Kean and Dr. Brookings, to make all the Dr. Kean lighting design setup evenings for the college production and not miss any rehearsals that included my multiple parts in *Once In a Lifetime*.

To this day, I remember with fondness the many evenings that just Dr. Kean and I worked late on the main stage, with him at his makeshift worktable at sixth row, center, in the audience and me in the booth at the light console. We were setting the light levels for all the instruments that determined the lighting design for the scene areas on the large stage. In some cases, Art (he let me call him by his first name) made notes for changing the color of some of the instruments (spotlight gels). Those cases required more work the next day when the full stage crew was available. A color change meant that one or more spotlights had to have their color gel changed before Art and I could resume the setting of light levels.

Once all the light-level settings were complete for all the scene areas, along with all the night or daylight varieties that had to be created, then the new levels were drafted into a detailed lighting-change script that I was to follow during each production night. And once Dr. Kean set the lighting-design script for all the scenes over the span of about ten evenings and preset the scenario for the lights among the dimmers, all that was left was for me was to follow the script. Pretty simple, huh? Not much artistic skill required. Well, the power this sixteen-year-old had over this university production never produced a dull moment.

My power trip at the controls on the console started with me dimming the house lights to signal the start of the performance. The console was full of sophisticated power-driven dimmers with multiple masters to control all the on-stage scene transitions. For me it was a perfect match of my love for the technical with my burgeoning love of the theater. I did not have the opportunity to pilot the *Enterprise* at warp 9 throughout the galaxy, but I was the only kid on the entire college crew. Wow! What a power trip! And this was *real*.

On opening night for *The Member of the Wedding*, I think I was more nervous in my new high-tech role as lighting master of the universe (at least at KU!) than I was as an actor in my various small roles in *Once in a Lifetime.*

"Beam me up, Scotty! Life doesn't get any better than this!"

Little did I know that this first real control console experience would be a key indicator and early theme of my upcoming life at a console of much more complexity and wide-reaching control within our solar system on the Apollo Program.

CHAPTER 2

Radio Station KIND (Console 2)

Abraham Lincoln's Gettysburg Address was partially responsible for helping me acquire my second control console job.

Back in Independence in 1960, at the end of my junior year in high school, my drama teacher and director of the school plays was Mrs. Margaret Goheen. She approached me one day in April to ask if I'd be willing to contribute to the city's Memorial Day services at the cemetery by delivering Lincoln's Gettysburg Address. I agreed and began memorizing the famous speech.

I found some of the passages rife with opportunities to add a little drama to Lincoln's words, so I looked forward to (perhaps) delivering a rousing version of his speech with gusto. In the end, I chickened out, because I realized that the words themselves carried their own weight of the sorrow of those Civil War dead.

As well, the somber tone of the ceremony at the cemetery discouraged me from too much drama. And, in thinking about it at the Gettysburg cemetery, I decided that Lincoln's words were just right if delivered clearly. So I toned it down some.

My voice projection level I still maintained so all could hear among the several hundred gathered that day. What I did not realize about the crowd was that everyone there had come mostly to pay tribute to a lost loved one. Perhaps some lost ones were also veterans of some war since the Civil War.

The words are stirring even today:

> Four score and seven years ago our fathers brought forth on this continent a new nation, conceived in liberty and dedicated to the proposition that all men are created equal.
>
> Now we are engaged in a great civil war, testing whether that nation, or any nation so conceived and so dedicated, can long endure. We are met on a great battlefield of that war. We have come to dedicate a portion of that field, as a final resting place for those who here gave their lives that that nation might long endure. It is altogether fitting and proper that we should do this.
>
> But, in a larger sense, we cannot dedicate—we cannot consecrate—we cannot hallow—this ground. The brave men, living and dead, who struggled here, have consecrated it far above our poor power to add or detract. The world will little note nor long remember what we say here, but it can never forget what they did here. It is for us the living, rather, to be dedicated here to the unfinished work, which they who fought here have thus far so nobly, advanced. It is rather for us to be here dedicated to the great task remaining before us—that from these honored dead we take increased devotion to that cause for which they gave the last full measure of devotion—that we here highly resolve that these dead shall not have died in vain—that this nation, under God, shall have a new birth of freedom—and that government of the people, by the people, for the people shall not perish from the earth.

Some phrases in the speech never die. I noticed that President-elect Obama paraphrased them in his acceptance speech on November 4,

2008: "a government of the people, by the people, and for the people has not perished from this Earth."

During my address, I first thought that I was being quietly interrupted at about the point of "We have come to dedicate a portion of that field as a final resting place for those who here gave their lives."

But I was wrong. It was not an interruption. A small chorus of sniffles was building in response to the power of those words. And I was a little shocked, so I adjusted my tone to finish on a quieter note. I had the personal satisfaction of what I thought was a reasonable repetition of President Lincoln's most famous words. I'm not saying that I am anything close to Abraham Lincoln in my delivery. It is just that those words are so powerful and that speech was so short and to the point. They instantly captured the tremendous sorrow of the day.

I stayed around after the program and greeted a few people I knew. I particularly remember the complimentary comments from my dad's boss, County Probate Judge David Scott.

Not long after that Memorial Day, I received a call from the owner of the local radio station KIND, Nelson Rupard. To my surprise, he asked if I were available to come in for an audition. Part of my surprise was that I had auditioned for him fifteen months previous and failed to get the job.

Of course I was available! If Mr. Rupard remembered my previous audition, he did not let on. What was the situation here? I first deduced that some of my fellow upperclassmen were going off to college. As they were KIND announcers, their departure perhaps created a new radio station vacancy. One of those departing gentlemen, who was two years my senior then, is now on TV for the Discovery/History Channel. He got his radio start at KIND. His name is Bill (Horton) Curtis. The other man is Hoite Caston. Both are regular contributors to the Discovery Channel. If I was to replace either of them at KIND, I had some big shoes to fill. Horton and Hoite were excellent announcers, in my opinion. Today Bill Curtis owns the station.

Our hometown was large enough to support only one radio station. And it was a small one. Its FCC class was termed "Sunrise-to-Sunset." And yes, that's when it was on the air, about 6:00 AM to 6:00 PM every day including weekends. Well, Mr. Rupard did not like to work weekends. And the station design was not too complicated. So he usually hired one low-cost student with technician skills (yours truly) for weekends, who could read the news on the air that came in off the leased Teletype wires of the Associated Press. I got the job at the grand 1961 salary of $1 per hour! Can you believe it? They actually paid me to become a radio star!

Later I learned that Judge Scott and Mr. Rupard were close friends. Then I put two and two together, genius that I was. That was one of my first lessons in the effect of personal influence and contacts in obtaining jobs. Purely the best qualifications were not the only factor in snagging the best job. I think I remember seeing Mr. Rupard in the cemetery crowd that day of my Gettysburg Address. Maybe he heard me firsthand that day. Or maybe he just agreed with his friend Judge Scott that my voice skills would suffice for his radio station. I'm not really sure.

I had to admit that I was not hired for my honey-toned radio voice or my acting skills, neither of which were on good display during my second audition. Perhaps one good Gettysburg Address had done it all!

That story turned out to be a great conversation piece. I have bragged all my life that I started out as a popular DJ in my hometown. I usually left out the part where the station was so powerful that its signal reached all the way to the city limits of Independence, Kansas! Oh well, I was getting experience in radio where I ran the whole station, usually by myself.

I'll never forget those station promos: "This is K-I-N-D, kind radio, ten-ten on your radio dial. The friendly voice of southeastern Kansas with studios in the Booth Building in *Independence*!" Still today I can drop into my special radio voice and rattle it off at the drop of a hat. The news came off the AP wire every hour, already pared to five minutes for me to read cold. I loved it all, being in total control!

I got to do it all on each full weekend. I think that is the first and last time that I ever "acted" while positioned in front of a console. Again, it wasn't the cockpit of Captain Kirk's *Enterprise* on *Star Trek*, but then I wasn't exactly traveling at warp 9 in Independence, Kansas.

How did a nerdy tech crazy kid like me fill up a weekend of professional radio? Well, it wasn't rocket science (yet). After a short training session with Mr. Rupard, I learned to find each day's schedule before signing on the station. I read most of the commercials (cold) as well as the news hourly with frequent time checks. I even had my own DJ show, but the station did not have a good library of music. Therefore, I was not able to build up a local fan base like I had hoped. Most of my classmates listened to other rock-and-roll stations that had all the latest sixties hits.

The great rock-and-roll stations broadcasted from the large cities, mostly from Tulsa (KVOO), Oklahoma City (KOMA), and Chicago (WLS). All were FCC Clear Channel stations with 50,000 watts of power (I kept it to myself that KIND had 500 watts!). My personal favorite was KOMA at 1520 in Oklahoma City. I even visited the station years later when I was driving through from Los Angeles on I-40, the original Route 66.

The broadcast console had all the comforts of a high-tech home, including gauges right in front of me to control and monitor volume. One add-on was very important, considering that Independence was right in the middle of tornado alley in the Midwest, where heavy thunderstorms frequently occurred. The addition was a rearview mirror, just like on a car. It focused on the transmission-signal-strength gauge behind me, which indicated whether or not I was on the air. During strong storms when I had to read the news, I made a point to stop briefly every few paragraphs to glance at the mirror. If the gauge read zero, I knew that I was off the air and wasting my breath, and it was time for Plan B. Plan B was my procedure for reinitiating the carrier signal to put me back on the air. During tornado season this happened often.

If I forgot to check it for a time then noticed the gauge was at zero, I was doubly frustrated. Not only was I off the air and depriving the world (really just the city) of my golden tones of intelligence, but also I was unaware of what time I lost the carrier. In that case I treated my vast audience with nearly a complete repeat of the newscast.

Most of the weekend was filled with preplanned shows. If I had been looking forward to becoming a famous local DJ with the entire weekend dedicated to my lively and popular show of shows crammed with great rock-and-roll, I was to be sorely disappointed. I did get one to two hours. The rest of each weekend was usually filled with shows like:

- Prerecorded national shows on tape.
- Live shows from remote locations.
- Live shows coming in by remote line.
- Prerecorded religious shows on Sunday morning from ministers.
- Prerecorded religious music by choirs and orchestras.

All that was required of me was "complicated engineering tasks," such as turning on a tape or opening a remote line. Even though I did not yet have my electrical engineering degree from KU, I was able to tackle these tasks with success.

I loved the challenge. I think it was the only job I ever had that combined my two great loves! Many extemporaneous reports were required from me, so I got to be an actor, and to add my own style to my DJ introductions of all that great rock-and-roll. Even my ad libs plunged to great depths with my groan-able jokes, most of them bad puns.

Example: "All I wanted was a bottle in front of me. And they gave me a frontal lobotomy!"

Example 2: "Someone asked the difference between ignorance and apathy. And I said, 'I don't, and I don't care!'"

Example 3: "Beam me up, Scotty. There's no intelligence here!"

Enough? Thought so!

My good friend and acting partner, at school as well as at the Lawrence Summer Stock, also had a radio show on the weekend. Her name is Gigi Gibson. Her show was live for one hour. I set up a room for her at the station and gave her a great introduction. Her well-planned show covered current events at the school as well as in the community. Gigi did a good job with it, and she made show business a lifelong career, mostly in New York City.

Gigi and I made a good team during those high school years. We found ourselves in many acting roles together on stage before we graduated. I guess our peak of accomplishment was our respective leading roles in the all-school production (both high school and junior college) of Tennessee Williams's *The Glass Menagerie.*

That's Gigi on the far right.

In addition, we both attended the two summer sessions at the KU summer theater program before we snagged our radio jobs in our senior year of high school.

Gigi continued in the theater business all her life, in contrast to this "techie" nerd. At a recent high school reunion in Independence, we both caught up with what each of us had done with our lives. She told me she evolved a successful acting career on the New York stage into a position on a New York State Commission with New York state theater budget authority.

Not only was the job at Station KIND a step up in my financial life, but it was also helpful in gaining more experience in live theater. Radio was an offshoot of my early interest in live theater from my two summers at KU. I was able to pursue some of this interest squeezed into a tight college engineering-class schedule. I tried out for a one-act play in my junior year in college and got a small part. Guess I didn't have the courage of Gigi to make it my profession for life. However, I made up for it somewhat with my involvement in community and regional theater later in Houston, working with up to fifteen different theaters in the Houston area.

That summer of 1960 flew past. Before I knew it, I was starting my senior year of high school and my last year living in Independence. My job at the radio station, with all the acting, ad libs, and technical tasks, was one of the greatest experiences of my life.

The year 1961, with my graduation in May, was filled with great theater and high-tech classes at the college level. It was also a milestone year for another person named Alan. The first manned spaceflight of an American into space, which started the U.S. space race, occurred that year, with a liftoff on May 5, 1961—right around the time of my high school graduation.

More important for the nation and my future was an event about ten days after Alan Shepherd's flight. President Kennedy was speaking to Congress. He announced the new goal of NASA and the American space program. It included "landing a man on the Moon and returning him safely to the Earth" before the end of the decade.

Given that Alan's lob-shot flight (no orbit yet) was a success on May 5 after many ICBM launch-vehicle failures at the Cape, the announcement was a shock to many. The inventor of Mission Control for those manned space missions was a man from Virginia named Christopher Columbus Kraft, my future boss and mentor. When he heard what the president said after Alan's flight, he responded with something like, "What the hell is that man talking about!"

And what a decade it was for NASA *and* me! After my high school graduation in 1961 in Independence, Kansas, the year 1969 found me in Houston for the Apollo 12 launch. My position was in the main control room of the Apollo Mission Control Center, with major subsystem operations responsibility. I remember Chris Kraft on occasion stopping by my Instrumentation and Communications Officer (INCO) console in the MOCR with an encouraging "Good luck, young man!"

I was not yet on the bridge of the starship *Enterprise*, but never mind. I was at the center of the NASA universe! This time, pretty close to reality, at least for our Moon in the solar system!

CHAPTER 3

The Fire (Console 3)

Me in Apollo Mission Control.

"Oh my God, we killed the crew!"

I don't remember who said it, but I agreed with the call. We all killed the crew of Apollo 1. Who do I mean by "we all"? Gene Kranz, Flight Director, made it clear to all of us flight controllers in Mission Control that fateful day in 1967 that we killed the crew. But in the larger sense every NASA or contractor person who was rushing his or her Apollo schedule to "catch up" was partially to blame including, as a minimum:

1. The flight crew: Gus Grissom, Ed White, and Roger Chaffee.
2. The Pad 34 launch team at the blockhouse.
3. The launch team at the Kennedy Space Center (KSC).
4. The flight controllers at MCC-H.
5. NASA management at all centers involved with Apollo, including NASA headquarters in Washington.

President Kennedy's goal of "landing a man on the Moon and returning him safely to the Earth" had just suffered its biggest setback of the decade.

Personally, I remember being really tired that week because of the long hours I had put in supporting four major pad tests over four long weeks. That support was just coming to a close in record time for so many major tests. I was fatigued from working to get those pad test procedures right and published and distributed. But I was not aware that other members of the launch support team were just as weary, if not more so. I guess that we, each in our own area of responsibility, were working too hard and cutting those forbidden corners, perhaps without knowing it.

My role for Flight Control Division was to help the launch team build the test procedures. Specifically, my task was to incorporate the relatively few MCC-H flight controller callouts over the four days of each test. The inputs from the Houston controllers were relatively small, but the books for the test were huge! They were so big that KSC had to divide them into two volumes for the major four-day tests that included the launch countdown and its final rehearsal, the countdown demonstration test. The total Operational Checkout Procedure (OCP) for each test was in two volumes of over a thousand pages each. Each was a full countdown in some form. The major activity was crammed into the last four hours when the launch vehicle was fully fueled (on launch day only) and the flight crew had entered the spacecraft to get positioned for launch by performing their final prelaunch checks.

That Friday was the last day of what was called the "Plugs Out" test. This test ended with the final countdown including flight crew positioned in their spacecraft, but with the hatch open. Note that the hatch was to be kept open. The spacecraft, which was the first manned Apollo mother ship, was called the CSM for Command Service Module. The CSM made the entire journey to the Moon and back, but left the landing part of the journey to the other spacecraft, called the LM for Lunar Module.

APOLLO COMMAND MODULE MAIN CONTROL PANEL

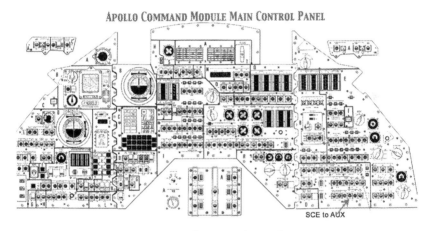

CSM cockpit switch panel.

The Plugs Out test did not include fueling the launch vehicle. The four-day countdown included mostly activity for the launch team to rehearse the actual countdown.

The MCC flight control team's role was limited and concentrated as a full team during the last day of the countdown. Our activity from Houston included events like digital commands sent to the Apollo spacecraft at the prescribed times. Also included were reports of MCC team "Go/No-Go" decisions made at milestones in the count, and at times verification of some telemetry parameters to the KSC launch team. That was my job before the test: Make sure these MCC events were correctly incorporated into the OCP documents at the correct time.

The Plugs Out test proceeded through all events for both launch and flight teams, except the fueling right up to the countdown end called T minus zero. For the launch to be successful, all the final Pad 34 connections between the launch tower and the space vehicle were required to be ejected just before ignition. These connections were made through the launch tower on swing arms, which are long platforms stretching from the launch pad to the launch vehicle and spacecraft that can be retracted from the launch vehicle at launch. They look like arms and carry all the lines and umbilicals to the launch vehicle at each level. Swing arm number five at the top also included a catwalk for the crew to walk to enter the spacecraft. The OCP called for most swing arms to automatically swing back from the launch vehicle just before liftoff. That is what the Plugs Out test demonstrated. And Plugs Out was the test we were running on that fateful day.

At T minus zero, simulated ignition in Plugs Out, all the remaining plugs (lines to the spacecraft and launch vehicle) were ejected from the vehicle on the five swing arms. The swing arms were then swung back just before liftoff would have occurred.

Looking back, I remember that for four days the test did not go well. There were many unplanned starts and stops. One reason was launch team fatigue from too many major tests leading up to the Plugs Out test that one week.

Another reason for the test troubles could be traced back to delivery of the CSM Block I, as the spacecraft was called. The CSM wasn't ready when it was shipped to KSC from its factory in Downey, California. Therefore, many workers were required to continue their unfinished tasks during the testing. This was neither good nor safe. The activity disturbed the flight crew after they entered the CSM at approximately T minus two hours forty-three minutes. In addition to the noise from the tasks, the voice communication loops for the crew were also faulty. We had trouble hearing both the flight crew on the comm channels to Houston and the local launch. I think the flight crew comment was something like, "How can we get to the Moon if we can't talk between three buildings?"

There were many other CSM problems, all documented by the Apollo 204 Accident Review Board.

At first I could not believe that the crew had caught fire. I knew the CSM environment was pure oxygen, but for this test the hatch was supposed to remain open. How did it get closed? There was only one way, I thought. Only one person had enough authority to override the safety procedures of the test: the Mission Commander, Gus Grissom. Gus must have reached the end of his patience with the loud noise going on around him both inside and outside the spacecraft that day. But it wasn't the fault of the launch team workers. The CSM was also behind schedule and shipped to the Cape from Downey, California, with much work yet to be accomplished. The remaining work was to be performed at the Cape during testing. It may have been a good idea at the time. But it did not work.

Even we flight controllers in Houston had complained on several occasions about the noise on the comm channels during Plugs Out.

Apparently some managers on the program had decided that the parallel work on the CSM must continue during the testing in order to make up some of the lost time in the schedule. The goal was to get back on the planned Apollo launch schedule in order to meet the goal of "landing a man on the moon before the end of the decade."

I recall the horror when the bodies of the crew were found at the hatch attempting to open it. However, the hatch opening required a long one hundred-second procedure designed to preclude inadvertent opening in space, which seemed like a good idea at the time.

Recently I recalled the words from astronaut John Young, who was quoted in the new movie *In the Shadow of the Moon*. John was a close friend of Gus and later Commander of Apollo 16. John said Gus had complained to him about the incomplete status of the CSM and all the work still in process during the testing. In Gus's opinion, there was too much work going on, and the CSM was not in very good shape with its myriad wiring changes.

John suggested at the time: "Complain to our chief and to NASA Apollo management that the work and test environment are unacceptable to you."

Gus's answer: "I can't. They'll just fire me and get someone else to fly the first Apollo." John did not agree, but said nothing.

The next week Gus was dead right. He had never uttered a word of complaint.

I am reluctant to blame Gus, because he paid the ultimate price. If he closed that hatch against the safety procedure, I think I know why he did it. While I was on console in MCC-H, I heard all the noise and communications interference in from the spacecraft in my headset. My guess is that Gus probably had decided to clear the workers from inside the CSM, and to risk closing the hatch in order to get the Plugs Out finished in a quiet spacecraft. The communications did clear up during the last portions of the test. I thought that they would never get that hatch open if they had to, since it took a good one hundred seconds to open if you were not in a panic. I thought about this event a lot in the ensuing weeks and months. Maybe, just maybe, Gus could have closed the hatch and not latched it. I was not that familiar with that hatch myself but surely Gus was aware of the danger from a pure oxygen environment. The thought of a flash fire in 100 percent oxygen was probably the furthest thing from Gus's mind in his rush to finish the Plugs Out test.

Alan Bean, in the movie *In the Shadow of the Moon*, was quoted as saying he was confused when he heard that the crew was lost. He didn't understand, of course, when he said, "How could you *lose* the crew? They are probably just taking a break at their beach house on the Cape." Alan was as stunned as we all were when he learned the truth.

Our Flight Director in Mission Control, Gene Kranz, was equally stunned and shocked. The next day, I remember, he got all of the flight controllers together and rightly told us that we had killed the crew. He explained (also quoted in Gene's book/DVD: *Failure Is Not an Option*) that many things in our own Houston facilities like the Mission Control Center were not working right: telemetry software, simulations software, internal voice comm loops, external voice comm loops, etc. And no one said "Stop!"

I'm not sure about the resolution of the other NASA elements that had failed Gus and his team that fateful Friday. But I was sure about the resolve of our team of flight controllers in Houston. Why?

Because of what Gene Kranz said to all of us: "Nobody said stop!"

Gene went on to say that he did not know about the rest of NASA, but he knew about us. We were at fault. We killed the crew!

"None of our procedures were ready, none of our software had any shelf life. None of our Houston systems were ready. Much of our software did not even work correctly. And no one said, 'Stop!'" Gene emphasized.

From that point forward, Gene instructed us to develop a new attitude toward everything we did. To motivate us to no longer be part of the problem, Gene directed us to write on our blackboard the two words to which we must aspire and become known: "Tough & Competent." We were never to erase these words from our blackboards. And we complied.

Those words stayed a long time on many blackboards in Building 30 and Building 45 at the Johnson Space Center in Houston. Those words still stick in my mind, even today. Did we ever erase them? Yes. I think we may have erased them just after July 20, 1969, when Neil Armstrong stepped onto the surface of the Moon at Tranquility Base.

In my view, and that of the Apollo 204 Accident Review Board, we were all trying to do too much on too tight a schedule.

Take the Plugs Out test, for example. Plugs Out was the third major four-day all-up back-to-back pad test that we were trying to finish that fateful Friday.

- The flight crew was tired.
- The KSC launch operations crew was tired.
- The Pad 34 prelaunch crew was tired.
- The MCC flight teams in Houston were not so much tired as feeling the pressure of the schedule.

The prior major pad tests already completed were Plugs In and the Flight Readiness Test. Next up was another four days of Plugs Out, to be followed by the Countdown Demonstration tests, both wet (using fuel) and dry (no fueling). In the wet test, all launch vehicle stages were fully fuelled and the countdown to T minus zero was exercised for all the operations teams including the flight crew.

Looking back on the day of the fire, as I do from time to time even today, I had a bad feeling when I finished my long shift on the Procedures console in the MOCR. In spite of all the communications problems, we seemed to be making our way through all the countdown sequences in the OCP toward the T minus zero end of the test. The communications had seemed to clear up for some reason. In retrospect I think I know why. Back then I thought I heard someone on the comm loops at KSC say something about a closed hatch.

I knew that was not right for Plugs Out, because it violated the pad safety rules about a closed hatch in a 100 percent oxygen environment. The spacecraft was full of pure oxygen and was a definite fire hazard. Even the smallest spark could have set it alight. Pure oxygen was the correct environment for a real launch at the time. It was gradually replaced with nitrogen during the launch phase to eventually reach the Earth mixture (fourth-fifths nitrogen, one-fifth oxygen). The hatch on this Block One spacecraft was in two pieces and took over one hundred seconds to open at best. This was a safeguard design to preclude accidental opening in space, of course.

(Note: the Apollo Accident Review Board recommended the subsequent change to the launch oxygen environment and the hatch before any Apollo manned flight.)

I dismissed the report I thought I had heard during Plugs Out. No one was allowed to close that hatch, let alone latch it. I was already trying to remember where I parked my car, as I was getting off shift and it was dark already.

Not long after I left Mission Control: "Fire!"

Although I never heard all the details from the Apollo 204 Accident Review Board, I am now sure that Gus, or one of the flight crew, closed that hatch, killing themselves when the alleged electrical short occurred in the pure oxygen environment. I concluded on my own—no one ever told me, and I never asked—that Gus must have overridden pad safety in order to hear the comm loops for test completion. He was the only one with the authority to overrule pad safety at the time. And I'll bet he was convincing, if confronted. I can hear him talking to the pad leader to this day.

The usual pad leader for all manned spacecraft missions was Guenter Wendt. And Guenter was a hard taskmaster. His experience stretched all the way back to the days he worked for Wernher von Braun in Germany, when Wernher was newly in charge as a young man on the V-2 rocket pads for Hitler as they rained the V-2 bombs on London. Except Guenter was not on Pad 34 on that fateful day. His book, *The Unbroken Chain*, explains that he was not yet on contract as pad leader for North American. Guenter had worked under contract for McDonnell Douglas, the manufacturer of the previous Gemini spacecraft. North American was the new spacecraft contractor for the Apollo spacecraft.

I have often thought that someone on the Apollo 204 Accident Review Board decided that those who died would not get the blame. The price they paid was high enough. It was never documented who closed the hatch that day.

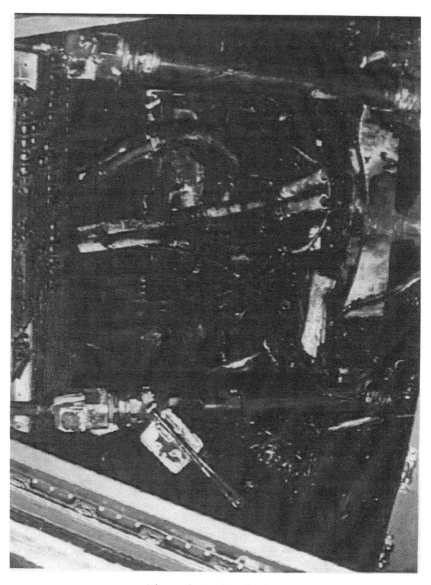

The cockpit after the fire.

From that day forth, from the perspective of my position in Mission Control, along with my prelaunch task of integrating those thousands of pages of OCPs, a new resolve grew in all of us. That resolve stretched all the way to Downey, California (a suburb of Los Angeles), where the Block II spacecraft were being redesigned and built to be safer. The centerpiece of the redesign was a new quick-opening one-piece hatch that could be opened with a seven-second procedure. "Tough & Competent" were still on every blackboard in Houston.

If we did not live up to those words, then we would not rise to the goal set for us by President Kennedy. Probably most of us in the Apollo Program throughout the country became painfully aware of that goal and those words. I had first heard the goal on the radio in 1961 as a senior in a far-off Kansas High School.

We did not have a lot of time to spare. Our task at NASA loomed large, given the time left in the decade to reach the Moon.

The biggest challenge was the need for a newly designed CSM. The Apollo 204 Accident Review Board decided early to move from the Block I developmental spacecraft to the newly designed Block II operational spacecraft, which contained the new quick-opening hatch, for the next flight. The new hatch was made of aluminum and fiberglass, which was enhanced by a gas-powered counterbalance mechanism, and could be opened from the inside in seven seconds and by pad safety crew in ten seconds.

The total list of recommendations from the Apollo 204 Accident Review Board was:

1. The amount and location of combustible materials in the Command Module must be severely restricted and controlled.
2. That the time required for egress of the crew be reduced and the operations necessary for egress be simplified.
3. Management continually monitors the safety of all test operations and assures the adequacy of emergency procedures.
4. All emergency equipment (breathing apparatus, protective clothing, deluge systems, access arm, etc.) be reviewed for adequacy.
5. Personnel training and practice for emergency procedures be given on a regular basis and reviewed prior to the conduct of a hazardous operation.
6. Service structures and umbilical towers be modified to facilitate emergency operations.

7. The Ground Communication System be improved to assure reliable communications between all test elements as soon as possible and before the next manned flight.
8. A detailed design review be conducted on the entire spacecraft communication system.
9. Test Procedures and Pilot's Checklists that represent the actual Command Module configuration be published in final form and reviewed early enough to permit adequate preparation and participation of all test organizations.
10. Timely distribution of test procedures and major changes be made a constraint to the beginning of any test.
11. Full-scale mock-ups in flight configuration be tested to determine the risk of fire.
12. The fire safety of the reconfigured Command Module be established by full-scale mock-up test.
13. Studies of the use of a diluent's gas be continued, with particular reference to assessing the problems of gas detection and control and the risk of additional operations that would be required in the use of a two-gas atmosphere.
14. An in-depth review of all elements, components, and assemblies of the Environmental Control System be conducted to assure its functional and structural integrity and to minimize its contribution to fire risk.
15. Present design of soldered joints in plumbing be modified to increase integrity or the joints be replaced with a more structurally reliable configuration.
16. Deleterious effects of coolant leakage and spillage be eliminated.
17. Review of specifications be conducted, 3-dimensional jigs be used in manufacture of wire bundles and rigid inspection at all stages of wiring design, manufacture, and installation be enforced.
18. Vibration tests be conducted of a flight-configured spacecraft.
19. The necessity for electrical connections or disconnections with power on within the crew compartment be eliminated.

20. Investigation be made of the most effective means of controlling and extinguishing a spacecraft fire. Auxiliary breathing oxygen and crew protection from smoke and toxic fumes be provided.
21. Every effort must be made to insure the maximum clarification and understanding of the responsibilities of all the organizations involved, the objective being a fully coordinated and efficient program.

With the extra time afforded the NASA operation teams because of the CSM redesign, many other elements of the program in Houston, KSC, and the worldwide Manned Spaceflight Flight Network (MSFN managed by the NASA Goddard Spaceflight Center) gained sufficient schedule time to do more of the right things in getting ready for Apollo 7, the new first manned Apollo flight.

After the fire at Pad 34, all the space vehicles were removed from the pad for analysis by the Apollo 204 Accident Review Board. Pad 34 was on the Cape Canaveral side of the Kennedy Space Center. The name of the Cape was changed to Kennedy a short time after the President's death. However, the Canaveral name was more popular with the locals, which prompted a name change back to Canaveral a few years later.

Most of the NASA buildings that made up the KSC were located on the Merritt Island side of the center. The new Apollo Saturn V launch pads, A and B, were on Merritt Island also, but much closer to the Atlantic Ocean. The new Apollo pads made up Launch Complex 39. (See Figure 7.)

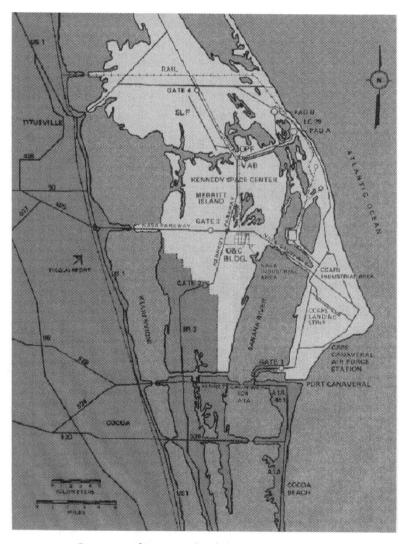

Overview of Merritt Island and Cape Canaveral.

Apollo launch operations were more complex than those for the initial ICBM launches across the Banana River at the older Air Force "Missile row" on Cape Canaveral. Pads 34 and 37 were part of Missile Row. Apollo 7 was to be the first launch of the redesigned Block II CSM using the smaller Saturn IB Apollo launch vehicle. (See Figures 8 and 9.) The Block I CSM became history and never flew in space with a manned crew as a result of the fire. NASA management decided to go directly to the Block II CSM spacecraft to gain time in the schedule.

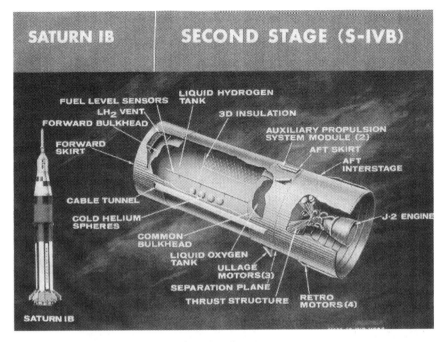

Saturn IB diagram.

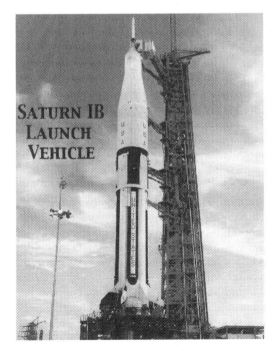

Saturn IB overview.

Apollo 7 was launched on October 11, 1968, marking a return to flight of the Apollo Program just eighteen months after the Pad 34 fire. The changes that resulted from the fire were accomplished in record time to put the Apollo Program back on a reasonable schedule that allowed the chance to achieve President's Kennedy's goal before the end of the decade.

Note New Quick-Open Hatch on the Left for Apollo 7.

In order to reduce support of any combustion, launch pad S/C cabin atmosphere for all pre-launch testing was now a mixture of 60% oxygen and 40% nitrogen instead of the 100% oxygen. The "enriched air" supplied by new ground equipment involved no hardware changes in the spacecraft. The Flight Crew suit loops, however, still carried 100% oxygen. After launch, the 60-40 oxygen-nitrogen mix was gradually replaced with pure oxygen until cabin atmosphere reached 100% oxygen at 5 psi. The enriched air mix was selected after extensive flammability tests in various percentages of oxygen at varying pressures.

Other Apollo Spacecraft changes were:

*Substituting stainless steel for aluminum in high-pressure oxygen tubing

*Armor plating water-glycol liquid line solder joints

*Protective covers over wiring bundles

*Stowage boxes built of aluminum

*Replacement of materials to minimize flammability

*Installation of fireproof storage containers for flammable materials

*Mechanical fasteners substituted for gripper cloth patches

*Flameproof coating on wire connections

*Replacement of plastic switches with metal ones

*Installation of an emergency oxygen system to isolate the crew from toxic fumes

*Inclusion of portable fire extinguisher & fire-isolating panels in the cabin.

I remember there was a healthy amount of the "go" momentum from all the teams involved in Houston and at KSC for Apollo 7. And the flight crew seemed to have an extra amount of determination—so much so that during the flight it triggered an argument between the flight crew and the flight team in Houston. The national news reported that we were just having a "spat" between the astronauts and the ground team at MCC-H.

Wally Schirra was Astronaut Commander of the flight. And the Flight Director (three shifts) on the ground in Houston was the overall leader of the mission, with all mission decision power. The head of all flight operations, Christopher C. Kraft, Jr., picked all the Flight Directors.

Dr. Kraft invented Mission Control and was not only a godlike figure to all the younger flight controllers, but also he was rising rapidly in the NASA hierarchy to gain and retain all management power over the missions. I provide this background to give you an idea of what transpired between Wally and Chris at the time of their spat out of sight of the national news.

As I recall we (the flight team on the ground in Mission Control) had asked the crew (Wally) to perform a procedure that was not documented in his flight plan. It was a last minute suggestion by someone on the flight team to provide more thorough flight information on one of the spacecraft's systems—propulsion, I believe. The crew had already completed the planned tests in the flight plan ahead of schedule, and these additional tests were determined to be a good engineering idea which added to the minimal flight data we had already received on the system.

However, Wally did not see it that way. He said something like he was not going to perform any procedure that was not part of the plan and was probably generated overnight by some jerk in the back rooms of Mission Control.

As a matter of fact, the engineering team from NASA and the CSM contractor in the MCC back room did generate the idea. But it was thought through and planned within the time then available for the mission and approved up our MCC chain of command, including Chris.

Well, Wally's words infuriated Chris like I had never seen. He was furious with both Wally, for those words, and the insubordination they implied. Donald K. (Deke) Slayton, an astronaut from the Mercury program who was then the Director of Flight Crew Operations under Chris, sided with Chris on this one. Not much else was to be said about the situation. In the vernacular of the time, Wally won the battle of the "spat" but lost the war of his astronaut career.

Wally was directed by Deke, his boss, to perform the procedure the next mission day. But the damage had been done, and Wally knew it. Not long after the mission, Wally retired from NASA and never flew again. I won't tell you what Chris said about Wally, but it had something to do with leaving him in orbit as he had nothing to return to at NASA on Earth.

Wally was not the only victim of this spat. The astronaut careers of all three Apollo 7 astronauts were over because of it. Why?

Dr. Kraft soon rose in the NASA organization to become director of the Johnson Space Center and one of the most respected men of the Apollo Moon Landing Program. And Dr. Kraft made sure that no member of the Apollo 7 flight crew ever flew in space again.

That was the negative end to a successful Apollo 7 mission. However, it paved the path for the Apollo Program to move toward its final goal before the end of the decade: Apollo 11.

CHAPTER 4

Speech Class as Introduction to Live Theater

Tenth-grade Speech class marked the beginning of my love of live theater. I selected Speech as an elective, not knowing what to expect—especially not discovery of the second great love of my life! Remember, science fiction had already become my first love, because it allowed virtual exploration of the universe through the great authors of the time.

What about my love for the opposite sex? By tenth grade, I was certainly aware of girls but had not yet developed the courage to break out of my shell and start a conversation or relationship with one. I was perfectly happy, or reasonably happy, with my first love. The theater experience, however, allowed me to overcome much of my shyness toward girls.

Speech class was taught by the wonderful Mrs. McAlester, who brought many hidden talents to this young class of rookies, especially in skills to get us on our feet. She felt that it was important to start conquering what is generally known as people's greatest fear: standing up in front of a group to speak.

I can't remember the speech subjects, but I do remember the preparation that I applied to the exercise in order to overcome my fear of the audience. I think I memorized a good amount of my first speeches. I remember being criticized as a little too stiff in my first deliveries.

Then the genius of Mrs. McAlester showed through. She brought us all together in the exercise that gradually became Speech Choir. The Choir, our class, became comfortable with the spoken word in unison, and most of our fears dropped away as we came to enjoy the group exercise of telling "speech choir" stories.

Assignments in Mrs. McAlester's class awakened in me some early talent and interest, but more than that. Up until then, I confess to being not only a bit of a nerd, but a quiet and shy one. Speech Class assignments ranged from membership in Speech Choir to individual presentations to the class. Our speeches involved reading and reporting on our own performance.

Studies still show that one of the greatest fears of anyone is getting up in front of a group to speak. To address this fear, our Speech Choir performed for a variety of groups in schools and the community. Because I was assigned multiple solos, my fear was eventually replaced with speaking skills that have stayed with me all my life.

Today I am still available for guest speaking engagements on a variety of space subjects, beginning with my Apollo experience. I advertise myself as one of the "original men of Mission Control." "Intelligent Life in the Universe" is also a favorite topic.

Mrs. McAlester directed our productions like a pro. Slowly but surely she assigned individual speaking parts, usually lines for a character in our stories to be delivered as a solo when the Choir became quiet. All these were well scripted in pieces already written for speech choirs. But what was great was the opportunity for an individual, within the comfort of the group, to add as much life and character as the teacher would allow. And, boy, was I ready for my lines! I can't believe how fast I became a full-fledged ham actor. I think I was one of the few Choir members that Mrs. McAlester had to bring down from a tendency to overact.

This experience was my initial, and very subtle (but clever), introduction to acting. I don't remember the details of all our performances, but almost everyone enjoyed them. Not everyone wanted individual parts to speak. But I sure did!

The experience of Speech Choir led naturally to reading for the tenth-grade production of a live play. Yes, I was hooked and tried out for a part. I don't remember that play like I should, but I do remember that I really enjoyed the entire process, from selection for a part to memorizing the lines, to blocking all the action for the scenes. I became more hooked with each step in the process.

As first I thought that memorizing my lines would be the most difficult part. That was a process you had to do on your own, and I preferred the get-togethers for rehearsals best of all. But I was such a precise nerd that lines came easily to me, particularly after the play's action had been blocked to go along with the dialogue.

I felt a little sad when the class came to an end. However, the end presented me with one of the greatest theater opportunities that I would ever have. That was the chance to attend the Midwestern Music and Art Camp at KU in Lawrence over six weeks of the summer, described in Chapter 1 and in more detail below. What an opportunity for a nerd was budding into a ham actor! Boy, did I need some special training to tone me down!

Still in high school, my next theater experiences were major school productions of a variety of plays popular at the time in the theater world. In eleventh and twelfth grades, I elected classes that included speech and drama with teacher Mrs. Margaret Goheen. Through my well-guided and dedicated efforts over those years, I came to love the performing arts as much as the nerd in me excelled in math and sciences. High points included playing the lead role in *The Glass Menagerie* by Tennessee Williams (along with Gigi and two other gentlemen), and winning the Anna Ingleman Supporting Actor Award (first one awarded; more about this below).

My first concentrated splash into the world of theater arts came in the summer of 1959. Five of us—Gigi Gibson, Irene Gibson, Hoite Caston, Bill Clement, and myself (selected by Mrs. McAlester, as I recall)—served a delightful six-week stint at the Midwestern Music and Art Camp. I'll never forget my first view of the KU Theatre. It was brand new in 1959 and filled with state-of-the-art of equipment and multiple stages, all designed for the theater-learning environment. Only the talent of the KU theater faculty surpassed the beauty of the theater itself. They stayed over the summer to teach and direct us young high school kids.

Each day was filled to capacity, mornings with stagecraft and acting classes and afternoons with stagecraft hands-on laboratories. Evenings were rehearsals for our production, *Once in a Lifetime*. That did not leave much free time except weekends. But we did not care. We were having the time of our lives with each other and the learning experience.

In Chapter 1, the story of my first console experience is one example of the meaningful work that I, as well as the rest of the theater group, experienced. My work with the lighting console would be key to many control consoles in the future, culminating at NASA Mission Control. My console in the main control room at Mission Control was not that much different in layout from my lighting control console at KU's University Theatre in 1959. However, in the one case I controlled stage lighting for a university production; in the other case, I monitored and controlled the Apollo manned spacecraft.

Our preparations for *Once in a Lifetime* at KU included several challenges for me. I was assigned a total of five small roles for which I had to learn the blocking and lines of dialogue, which I had to blend with my lighting console job and rehearsal schedule. Evening rehearsals included the entire cast of twenty-five people working on the many scenes and segments. Our performance on the University Theatre main stage was the highlight of our summer's work. The show was successful, thanks in large part to our University faculty and director, Dr. Jack Brookings. He was also the official head of our high school theater group for the summer.

When our six weeks ended, we had a difficult time saying good-bye to each other. The camp provided a yearbook of our experiences, with many pictures from our production. We used our yearbooks to record our heartfelt experiences and to sign personal notes in everyone's book.

When I attended KU later in 1961 after graduating from high school, I was embarrassed when I encountered Dr. Brookings. He asked where I had been, and I answered with my major: electrical engineering. A student engineer is not what he expected to hear from me! Given that we had had two intense summers together in the theater division, he'd expected me to stay with theater education. I'm sure he felt my training and budding talent at his hand were wasted if I became an engineer. He was complimentary regarding my talent potential. And later in life, after college, I did use that talent in many ways. My Midwestern Music and Art Camp experience added measurably to my lifelong talent in and love of live theater in many venues. My later work on many community theater stages, some TV commercials, and guest speaking for NASA Apollo attest to the value of that early training. But at the time, encountering Dr. Brookings, I could not see into the future. He seemed disappointed in my answer. I tried to console him with compliments about the life-changing experience I had gained from him, but to little avail.

During my engineering studies in junior year, I finally found time in my busy study schedule to try out for a play at the KU Experimental Theatre. I won a small role in a small avant-garde production entitled *Oh Dad, Poor Dad, Mama's Hung You in the Closet and I'm Feelin' So Sad.* I played the part of a bellboy, which did little to challenge my abilities at the time, but at least I was back in the theater business.

As a senior in High School I was returning from camp with what I thought was a greater knowledge of live theater crafts. My senior year was destined to blossom in three venues:

Lead role in *Glass Menagerie* on the stage

Gettysburg Address at Memorial Day city cemetery services

DJ/Engineer on KIND local radio station, "1010 on your dial"

Refer to Chapter 2 above for a description of obtaining my radio job, and how it evolved from my delivery of the Gettysburg Address on Memorial Day at the cemetery. The Speech and Drama director of our high school was also the same director for the junior college. That came about from the unique combination of the last two years of high school co-located with the junior college. This allowed the high school students to benefit from the college teachers. Most of them had a master's degree in their respective fields.

Mrs. Margaret Goheen was our speech and drama teacher and director for the production of *The Glass Menagerie*. I read for the lead role of Tom Wingfield and was lucky enough to be chosen. My friend Gigi Gibson, a senior, was also cast. The other three parts were cast with junior-college students. Gigi and I were the only high school students in this production. We were also colleagues on Radio Station KIND. The play is a classic, and we brought the right amount of respect and effort to each of our roles, making for a successful production. The reviews were good for all cast members as well as for the overall play. Mrs. Goheen was very pleased. My role was the narrator of this autobiographical saga. That meant a lot of lines to learn. I thought I did a respectable job with the role, and the kind reviewers did also. But the most important goal for me was to create the character that Mrs. Goheen required. She told me later during the production run that I had accomplished that goal to her satisfaction.

As it happened, the lead character was a heavy smoker. That was my only reservation. I didn't smoke. The play called for smoking through the duration of the long narratives. I was at a loss as to how to solve this. The director allowed me to fake it by holding a lighted (by someone else backstage) cigarette. I was sure someone would catch me faking it, because I did not know enough about the techniques of holding and flipping ashes the way a real smoker does. I guess I pulled it off. I concentrated on putting more research and effort into the right emotion for all the narratives. It was not easy, and I had a bad time of it. Some of my close friends knew I didn't smoke and caught me faking it a few times. I grew up in a house full of smoke that was hanging in the air all during my boyhood, which is probably why I never had the desire to smoke and don't to this day. I must have pulled it off because I received excellent reviews. The play was successful, and the whole cast did a respectable job with the difficult drama.

That wasn't the end of my high school acting. The college directing class project did plays chosen by the class students. High school students were cast in each production. I read for a small part in a one-act play directed by Sharon McAlester, daughter of my tenth-grade Speech teacher who launched my love of the stage. The play was an avant-garde production entitled *The White Lawn*. My small part was more fun than work, with few lines to learn. Nevertheless, I tried to do a reasonable job with the minor character. Apparently I did, as I received an Anna Award for Best Supporting Actor. The award was named after Anna Ingleman, drama teacher of the famous playwright William Inge.

After my numerous performing roles as a senior, my talent, such as it was, took a back seat to my KU education in engineering.

CHAPTER 5

Senior Star: Stage, Radio, and Community

With a freshman scholarship to KU in hand, I left my hometown to embark on my college engineering education and eventual career. My sustained effort, driven somewhat by fear of failing to make the grade, paid off at the end of my freshman year. I was awarded a full scholarship including all tuition and fees for my sophomore year.

Chapter 2 traces my dramatics to the cemetery at Independence. No, I didn't die on stage. I wasn't Abraham Lincoln, either, but I gave his Gettysburg Address a good college try at the Memorial Day service. I can trace that performance all the way to my radio station KIND job for the duration of my senior year.

The year 1961 was a full one for me. I think I did a little maturing, at least in the areas of jobs, classes, plays where I was the lead, and preparing for college.

In a small town like Independence, the normal education path for most seniors was to spend the first two years of college right there at home, in junior college. It was available in town and we knew the teachers already because they were also our high school teachers. The co-location of the two schools provided several advantages.

For example, the nerd in me jumped at the chance to take college classes during high school. Our senior high school classes were in the same building as the classes for the Independence Community College

(ICC). Therefore, when one's high school credits for graduation were met, one could substitute any of the available ICC classes. I learned that a freshman in Engineering School at KU started off in the math area with calculus, based on the assumption that you had completed college algebra and trigonometry classes in high school. If not, they were offered at KU. But taking them in college put you a full semester behind in the four-year engineering curriculum. That's why I jumped at the chance to take college algebra and trigonometry during my senior year.

Another advantage of the combined schools was that all our high school teachers were accredited at the college level. I already knew the math instructor, Mr. Boisdrenheim, well, having received A's in his high school algebra classes. And yes, this math nerd aced the two courses for college credit.

It was not a big surprise when I was accepted to KU. As a state university, KU was required to accept all students, with qualifying grades, from an accredited Kansas high school. My grades, including the five hours of college math classes, were all A's.

The second letter from KU, which granted me the KU Scholarship Hall Award, was the tipping point as to whether going there would be financially feasible. Unlike other scholarships, this one required me to pay for room and board. It included the cost savings to KU of my assigned chores in the hall as the major part of the award.

How can a scholarship require a payment? That monthly payment was a grand total of approximately $44 per month. That's what I paid in room and board for the privilege to live in Jolliffe Scholarship Hall. The difference between that $44 and the normal price for room and board at any residence hall or fraternity made up the amount of the award in cost savings to KU. The association with all the other men at the hall who were top grade achievers was no small advantage. There was no extra charge for the brain trust in each hall.

So the total school year charge for my room and all my meals was approximately $396. The savings between that value and the normal price for room and board was value of the scholarship. Depending on where you might choose to live in Lawrence, the value could range up from $675 for a room in a private home. But that included eating mostly cheap hamburgers. Residence halls and fraternities cost much more. The work in the Scholarship Hall included cooking meals and maintaining a clean residence. This saved the University hall upkeep and maintenance. It was a win-win situation for all concerned.

I loved it for the ease of work. I performed the duties of a waiter for most of my two years there. I also gained from the ready access to upperclassmen who had completed the engineering courses. Many of my colleagues already had good study habits and set a good example. Also, many had a little nerd in them, just like me.

As a sidelight, I had never enrolled in any foreign language classes during high school. And the Engineering School at KU had no foreign language requirements for graduation. So I thought I was home free regarding the challenge of any foreign language. However, like many things in life, that "success" caught up with me in 1988, when I accepted a position in Europe and moved there. My assignment to consult for the European Space Agency (ESA) was located at two space centers where members of the fourteen nations comprising ESA were based. (Chapter 8 covers this in more detail.) Once in Europe, I applied myself as best as I could to learning the local language. But I never became fluent in either German or Dutch. My only saving grace was that English was the required language at each of the ESA space centers.

One of my ways to compensate for lack of language skills was to make fun of Americans when I got the chance. My European colleagues enjoyed teasing us with American jokes; the most popular was the multilingual joke, the one where if trilingual is a person who speaks three languages, and if bilingual is one who speaks two languages, what do you call a person who speaks one language? An American!

My lame response was a joke on Texas. I claimed I knew what a *faux pas* was. Of course, that is a hole on a golf course in Texas that takes four strokes.

Back to 1961, my year of high school graduation. Earlier I mentioned that the decade of the Sixties got off to a fast start for me. As the school year was reaching its close, with me armed with theater, radio, and college class skills, the American space program was about to reach its first space-race milestone: the May 5, 1961, launch of Alan Shepard in his tiny one-man Mercury capsule.

The decade was a fast one for me as well as most Americans, with many outstanding results by decade's end in spite of all the American difficulties like the Vietnam War. My brother George became a Vietnam veteran because his chosen major at Kansas State University did not come with a deferment for his profession, as did mine.

I listened to this science fact, no longer science fiction, on the school radio. On May 19, 1961, President Kennedy injected the space race with some much-needed adrenaline by announcing the Moon as a goal of the new space agency, NASA. Starting as a young high school senior in 1961, I entered the fast track from honor graduate to a key career position, rising to become a member of the flight control team at Apollo Mission Control, Houston.

I was reminded recently in reading about the life of Paul Newman that he and I had a small connection that stretched from Houston's Clear Creek Country Theatre in 1968 all the way back to 1953 in New York; and forward to Beverly Hills, California, in the home of William Inge, Pulitzer Prize-winning playwright for *Picnic*. Mr. Inge's first home was Independence, Kansas.

The thread starts when William Inge first staged his play *Picnic* on Broadway in 1953. It was/is a classic love story based in Independence during Neewollah (Halloween spelled backward). The story begins when Hal arrives in Independence to visit Alan, his old college friend. Hal wants a steady job working for Alan's father, but his rough manners and good looks get him into trouble right away with his attraction to Madge who is Alan's finance. Meanwhile Millie, Madge's younger sister, adores him. He also catches the eye of Rosemary, a teacher who rents a room from their mother. In the end, Madge cannot resist her attraction to Hal. She breaks off her engagement with Alan. Madge and Hal leave town, intending to marry.

To this day the real Neewollah is celebrated in Independence. But I am getting ahead of myself.

Back in 1953, the part of Alan was filled by an unknown actor at the time, named Paul Newman. As the story goes, the part of Hal Carter was filled by the taller Ralph Meeker. But Paul requested that he play the cool drifter, Hal. His request was turned down by the renowned director Joshua Logan, allegedly because Paul Newman was not cool enough. (Could this be the only time in Paul Newman's life when he was *not* cool enough?)

In 1968, I played the part of Alan Seymour in Inge's play. Growing up in Independence, I never had the opportunity to meet the famous playwright. When *Picnic* won the Pulitzer in New York, I had just turned ten years old. But my mother, during the war years, I heard later, had the opportunity to act with Bill (Mr. Inge) at the old Independence Air Base theater.

When, in 1970, I telephoned Bill while I was in Los Angeles, the first thing I said to him was that my name is Alan Glines and I am the son of Mary Ellen (Patty) Glines with whom he acted at the Air Base back in 1941. That broke the ice between two strangers, and I was invited over to Mr. Inge's home in Beverly Hills for a fantastic afternoon. To this day I think that my mother named me

Independence is getting a lot of free publicity down at Houston these spring days and nights. The Little Theatre is producing our BILL INGE's Pulitzer prize-winning play "Picnic."

ALAN GLINES of here, who is a flight controller with the National Aeronautics and Space Administration, plays the part of "ALAN SEYMOUR." It's been so long since we've seen "P i c n i c" we forget which part that is.

Anyway, it was soon learned he hailed from BILL INGE's hometown, the locale for "Picnic". Consequently he's been beseiged with questions, including the radio and TV stations, on what he knows about Independence, Neewollah which figures prominently in "Picnic", INGE and anything else he has to offer.

INDEPENDENCE REPORTER NEWSPAPER CLIPPING MAY, 1968

Getting back to ALAN, according to ALAN's proud dad CLAIR, he's naturally on friendly terms with the astronauts. JOAN ALDRIN, the wife of BUZZ ALDRIN who is one of the Gemini 12 astronauts, also has a role in "Picnic". ALAN has been a guest in their lovely home.

Hometown newspaper clipping.

after Bill's *Picnic* character, Alan. Either him or Alan Ladd, a movie star she always admired.

How did Mom know that I would not grow up to be cool? Oh well ...

Back to 1968: I did not follow in Paul Newman's footsteps by demanding that I get to play the cool Hal. At the Clear Creek Country Theatre, the part of Hal was already cast with a very competent and cool actor, David McCormick. As I recall, my characteristic of being spaced out did not extend to fantasy—thinking I was as cool as Ralph Meeker, Paul Newman, or David McCormick. Does that make me too earthbound and normal? Hope not.

I did have the privilege of working with a Broadway actress named Joan Aldrin. She was Equity from the New York stage and did a superb job with the role of the drunken spinster schoolteacher named Rosemary, played with classic aplomb by Rosalind Russell in the film version of *Picnic*. The movie was also successful and starred William Holden as cool Hal and the beautiful Kim Novak as Madge, the girl who fell for him. A famous romantic scene I will never forget was when Hal and Madge slow-danced into the hearts of America during what was a Neewollah evening dance. Alan was seen off to the side as he developed a helpless, slow burn of jealous frustration. Most who saw the movie will never forget that scene between William Holden and Kim Novak, I think.

I was a guest in the home of Buzz and Joan Aldrin long before I knew Buzz. Buzz flew first on Gemini 11 before he was selected for the Apollo 11 mission, first to land on the moon. Joan had the cast and crew over to her home during the run of *Picnic*.

For my visit to Bill Inge's home in Beverly Hills, I came prepared. In addition to several copies of his plays, I brought his two modestly successful novels at the time. These gave me quite an armful!

Bill struck me as a quiet and reserved gentlemen. Of course, I was a little overwhelmed to be in his presence, given his success to date. I remember trying to catch him up on as many events from Independence as I could. Afterward, I decided that I had talked too much. I did share with him that during my last year in school I was honored with the first Anna, the Anna Ingleman Memorial Award. Anna Ingleman was the drama teacher at the Independence Junior College when Bill Inge was a student. Under her guidance, Bill began his lifelong career of dramatic writings.

My Anna acting award.

One of the plays Bill autographed was on loan to me from the Country Playhouse. Upon return to Houston, I read for a part in *Come Back, Little Sheba*. When I was cast, I requested from the director, Nancy Love, that I be returned the copy that I had checked out.

"Why?" she asked.

"Bill signed that copy to me a few weeks ago," I replied.

Nancy knew I was a smart aleck, and the tone of her answer revealed it. Yes, I had worked for her as a (self-centered) actor previously. So convinced was she that my story was fabricated that it took weeks to convince her I really had visited the real William Inge, famous playwright, through a connection from our mutual hometown. I finally had to show her one of my clippings that authenticated that I was from Independence, the setting of *Picnic*. I also showed Nancy some of the other items Bill had signed for me. She was impressed.

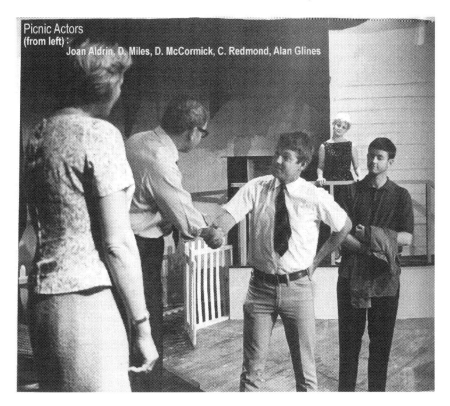

Picnic Actors
(from left) :
Joan Aldrin, D. Miles, D. McCormick, C. Redmond, Alan Glines

Picnic scene with Alan on the right and Joan Aldrin on the left.

Again, I am getting ahead of myself. Back on campus at KU, I applied all my new study habits to completing my degree. My only diversion from classwork presents an interesting story.

At one engineering enrollment period, I had to explain why an engineer was taking upper-division English classes. When I showed my advisor that an A average in English 1 and 2 allowed me to take "Introduction to the Drama," he understood even though he was surprised. He said it was good that some engineers could read and write!—then approved me for the drama course in the English department.

For my junior year, I dropped the Scholarship Hall Award and decided to live on my own in a room in a private home. I had my trusty (and new) 1956 Ford just purchased from my summer wages on a small Kansas pipeline project. But I needed a way to afford my new lifestyle. Three jobs were the answer. I turned my previous waiter skills into working as a busboy at a women's dormitory, Lewis Hall. Also I programmed in FORTRAN for the math department. And I helped out in one of the Engineering School labs.

I confess that I succumbed to the temptation of many students with multiple jobs and got a little greedy. I found a way to perform two jobs at once: bussing and programming. I found time during a slow period of busboy activity to program a little FORTRAN. And I continued this two-for-one activity until the day I was caught by the kitchen supervisor. My busboy tasks suffered a little, of course. But getting caught was the end of the practice for me. I played it straight with all three jobs for the remainder of the school year.

CHAPTER 6

My Path to the Cosmos via NASA
(A Journey in Seven Parts)

Part 1: My Turn to Interview NASA

Senior year at KU was the time to look ahead to a career. Job interviews with an assortment of companies looking to hire new graduates were made available to seniors in the School of Engineering. I signed up for a good number of interviews, looking for a job that would lead to a career. Regional as well as national companies were looking to hire many new engineers at the time of my graduation in February 1966.

But I was looking at NASA, which was hiring engineers into government jobs. Through research I discovered that all NASA jobs were Civil Service grades. These grades did not have starting salaries as high as offers from private industry, but I was still interested. My focus was the new space center in Houston, called the Manned Spacecraft Center (MSC). That was where Mission Control was managing the Gemini Program.

I followed the procedure to get on the Civil Service hiring lists for my grade (GS-7). But that put me on the lists for all GS-7 government jobs. In that sense, I may have overdone it. I received a total of twenty-seven job offers, mostly GS-7 grade, from around the country. Some were from private industry. But the most important to me were the one or two offers from every NASA center in the country. My primary interest was still the new space center in Houston, although I did consider the positions offered at the three primary NASA operations centers: Kennedy Space Center in Florida, Goddard Spaceflight Center in Maryland, and the Flight Research Center in California.

My final decision was the Manned Spacecraft Center (later the Johnson Space Center) in Houston. However, I had yet another decision to make. I had two offers in hand from MSC: one from Flight Control Division and one from the Flight Support Division. Neither was a direct connection to a flight controller position in Mission Control, but both had work directly related to tasks in Mission Control. I decided I needed more data. I contacted both position representatives and arranged to interview each in person. From the Flight Control Division interview, I learned that the position involved the training of flight controllers. From the Flight Support Division interview, I learned that the position involved working directly on the Gemini Digital Command System in Mission Control, making and validating all the commands that were transmitted to the Gemini spacecraft to effect some control of systems.

They approved my interview trip when I explained my dilemma. As Civil Service did not pay for recruiting trips at the time, I decided to pay the cost of my trip to Houston myself. I thought it was a worthwhile investment in my career. I did mention to each NASA person that my goal was to reach a decision on one of the two positions. In this sense I was interviewing NASA as much as they were interviewing me. My final decision was for the Flight Support Division (FSD), and I was hired into what became a very exciting position involving interchanges with many of the flight controllers. I hoped to someday become one of them, which came about in later years.

Part 2: Gemini DCS Tapes Go Worldwide

My initial assignment in the FSD was to assemble the Gemini Digital Command System (DCS) tapes. These tapes contained all the DCS commands to be transmitted to the Gemini spacecraft from the ground computers. They evolved for each Gemini mission and had to be updated and copied for each tracking site command computer. They were made of very strong material called Mylar. A copy was required for each Gemini remote-site computer for each mission. At the time, the sites with a command computer numbered ten worldwide.

The DCS tapes were assembled at the Master DCS computer on the second floor in Mission Control. That was my task. All the flight controllers were on the third floor and the mission computers were on the first floor. Starting with Gemini 8, after initial training, I assembled and checked out all the tapes for the sites around the world.

Neil Armstrong, Commander of Gemini 8, and I had slightly similar and parallel paths in 1966. His first spaceflight on Gemini 8 was my first mission supporting to the back rooms of Mission Control. While Neil was dealing with a stuck thruster in space, I was trying hard (as a green Kansas University graduate) to act like I deserved to be in Mission Control.

I was no longer green when Neil and Buzz stepped onto the surface of the Moon on July 20, 1969, during Apollo 11. I had ascended, not to the Moon, but to the position of INCO in the main control room of Mission Control. I had come far in my career by the end the decade!

With the early ending of Gemini 8, all the flight controllers deployed around the world returned to Houston. The Gemini 9 next mission could not be moved up in the schedule; therefore a gap of several months appeared in the schedule, which NASA management decided to fill by keeping flight controllers current. That involved a trip to and exercises at the Corpus Christi remote tracking site. The tasks would allow Gemini rehearsals to fill our gap.

I was selected to make the trip in support of my DCS command tapes. This was my first business trip with NASA flight controllers, and I was excited. I joined a remote site team in Corpus and got great operations experience from the rehearsals. I also made some lifelong friends on that trip in flight controllers Bob Legler and Joe Fuller. The rehearsals exercised my mission DCS commands in many of the mission procedures, both planned and contingency, in preparation for the next Gemini mission. This was my first direct association with flight controllers, and I learned much about spaceflight operations on the trip. Thanks to Neil Armstrong's broken thruster, I received a firsthand taste of flight controller operations. The head operator position at the site was called a TX CAPCOM (for capsule communicator) and was manned by Bill Garvin. He led the team in rehearsals of a tracking site pass. The technology of the time required flight controllers and CAPCOM at each site in addition to the primary team in MCC-H.

The decade had started with me as a high school senior and the space race getting underway. Space coverage came on the radio in 1961; at that time, television was around but most families in the town did not yet own one. The school was wired for announcements as well as radio when some national event warranted broadcasting to the entire school. That happened on May 5, 1961, with the launch of a guy named Alan was lobbed into space for the first time for this country in his tiny Mercury capsule. "Outer" space was a bit of an exaggeration, because his flight did not even achieve Earth orbit. However, the space race was on and we, the USA, were already behind. A Russian had achieved a space flight just a few weeks earlier. And our young President was not about to slow down.

Our fledgling space program had started off with many dramatic launch vehicle failures in front of the press with rolling cameras. Perhaps the Russian program had started the same way, but their lack of press coverage did not allow the world to see any of their failures. Only when Yuri Gagarin had successfully reached space did the Russians announce their success and provide the video after the fact.

Back to my twelfth-grade class on May 5, 1961. Alan Shepard's flight, coupled with my prolific science fiction background, was a watershed event in my life. Others were to come in a few short years. The decade of the 1960s had begun with a blast for me from Cape Canaveral, and my progress was to some extent parallel that of the nation for the remainder of the decade.

Even though many negative events were to try to dominate the nation, the space race stayed alive until we surpassed the Russians and achieved President Kennedy's goal of a man on the Moon and back by the end of the decade. The many events are well chronicled in a book by Tom Brokaw titled *Boom! Voices of the Sixties.* It is focused on the Baby Boomers (children officially born January 1, 1946) coming of age about then with all their challenges. As a War Baby myself (1943), my challenge was focused not so much on the Vietnam War and other events, but on the space race, which was to dominate my life.

President Kennedy's announcement on May 19, 1961, of a round trip to the Moon as a goal for NASA came about the same time I jumped on my fast track to the cosmos. By Presidential decree, NASA was also officially on the same fast track. One could say we were destined to join forces. How fast was that track?

In 1961, I monitored Alan Shepard's flight on radio from my high school class as a senior. By 1966, I had graduated with my bachelor's degree in electrical engineering (BSEE, it was called)—just in time for NASA's major hiring for its space programs. I got lucky there, as my preparation met up with the right opportunity.

With a little research into Civil Service I managed to get on the national hiring list at the time. That event allowed me to exceed the usual on campus hiring to the extent of a total of 29 job offers, mostly from NASA. As a matter of fact I received a job offer from every NASA center in the Country and two from MSC in Houston and the Kennedy Space Center (KSC) at the Cape. MSC was the newest (and closest to me) NASA center at the time with the name of the Manned Spacecraft Center (MSC). As a political sidelight, it turns out that Lyndon Johnson got Rice University to donate the land for MSC free of any cost. I joined the new MSC center in Houston and merged my personal fast track with NASA's. Through much focused effort, I rose to a key senior position in the main control room in Mission Control by 1969.

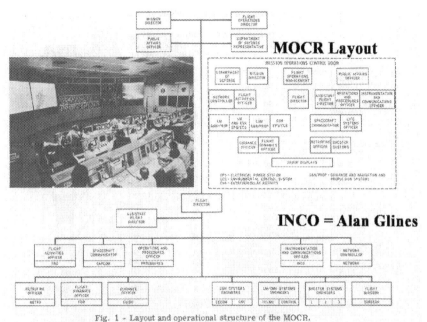

Fig. 1 - Layout and operational structure of the MOCR.

Apollo Mission Operations Control Room Overview

MOCR layout and chain of command.

I was part of an incredible team just beginning to rack up a large number of outer space accomplishments. Who were the young nerds in this brand-new Mission Control?

The original Mission Control was located in Florida at a Cape Canaveral blockhouse. It controlled all Mercury flights and the first two Gemini spacecraft flights.

John Aaron from Oklahoma is a good example of our team in Houston. He came to NASA much as I did, and became one of the truly great flight controllers of all time. He recounted his adventures on a 2005 Discovery Channel special about Apollo 13 entitled *Failure Is Not an Option.*, a TV version of Gene Kranz's book previously mentioned. Just ask Neil Armstrong (Gemini 8 and Apollo 11) and Alan Bean (Apollo 12 and Skylab 2) about John.

But I am getting ahead of myself again. John and I were both new flight controllers on the Gemini 2 manned spacecraft program, and both of us were overpaid (we thought) by NASA. How much? Our starting salaries from Civil Service were $7,304 per annum. But we always made more than that. Our NASA duties in Mission Control required much overtime in our quest for the Moon. And most overtime was paid. For me, that sure helped pay off those college loans I had accumulated at KU!

I did outdo John in one area. When seeking employment, he just wrote one letter inquiring about positions at NASA in Houston. He said he was shocked upon receiving, not information on positions, but a firm offer of employment at a salary that was "quite a shock to an Oklahoma country boy." This contrasts with my fast-track plan, which had led me to research the Civil Service process for hiring. Armed early with knowledge, I was able to use my BSEE to get listed for Civil Service employment upon graduation, which put my name on all U.S. government hiring lists. As I related above, this resulted in many offers, including at least one from each NASA center in the country. Two offers each came from MSC in Houston and the KSC in Florida, my favorites. I selected the right one and thereby met John.

My aunt Wilma, a close relative from Tulsa, Oklahoma, who played a big part in my early years, visited Mission Control sometime after the Apollo 13 mission. After meeting some of our team, she decided her favorite description of us pertaining to our Apollo 13 Presidential Medal of Freedom was the phrase "disciplined intelligence."

Apollo 13 Presidential Medal of Freedom.

Parts 3 and 4: My Transfer to Flight Control Division SSR Jobs

My tasks for the FSD were destined to be short-lived after the Gemini Program ended. So when an opening in the Flight Control Division (FCD) was advertised informally to me, I jumped at it. The FCD was exactly where I wanted to be since leaving KU. I applied to the Flight Control Operations Branch (FCOB) for the position and was interviewed. I got the position and transferred quickly from FSD to FCD, FCOB branch.

The chief of FCOB was none other than Gene Kranz, a Flight Director, who was to become my mentor. Gene was the most dynamic of the three Flight Directors at the time. The other two were Christopher Kraft, head of all flight operations, and John Hodge, chief of FCD. Gene's branch staffed two positions in the MOCR. The two were Assistant Flight Director and Operations & Procedures Officer. Additional support positions were stationed in the Flight Director Staff Support Room (SSR), or "back room" as it was called.

My assignment in FCD was twofold. The first was a coordination position off-console in the office. The second put me in a support position in the SSR for the operation and all rehearsals leading up to each mission. Both were exciting and placed me right where I wanted to be, supporting all the mission operations.

In the first task, I was assigned to John Temple. The two of us represented the Apollo Test Integration Working Group, or ATIWG as it was known. The ATIWG meetings were located at the Kennedy Space Center and required our attendance. This meant travel to KSC every two weeks for us both. The purpose of the meetings was to integrate all the operations elements into the procedures for all KSC testing of the spacecraft and launch vehicle on the pad for each mission. Some tests on the spacecraft were located in the building at KSC where the spacecraft first arrived, called the Manned Spacecraft Operations Building (MSOB). Testing included all the large all-up tests up to and including the launch countdown. The test procedures were called TCPs for Test Checkout Procedures and included primarily the launch team activity for the spacecraft and multistage launch vehicle. John and I inserted the flight team items and callouts for the flight team in MCC-H. The callouts were for every major test that required the Houston team. The tests the flight team supported from Houston included Plugs In, Plugs Out, Software Integration Test, Flight Readiness Test, Countdown Demonstration Test, and Launch Countdown.

At the end of the countdown and vehicle launch, the KSC launch team was in charge. At tower clear on each mission, the launch team handed over mission control authority to the Houston flight team. The Houston team in MCC-H was the control authority throughout the mission until splashdown at the end of the mission. In order to be ready to take control at tower clear, the Houston team and MCC-H systems were required to be all up and configured to accept handover during Launch Countdown.

The Software Integration Test was the only test at KSC where Houston was in charge of all testing. That test exercised all the digital commands from Houston to the spacecraft. A similar test exercised all launch vehicle commands. The tests assured that all commands performed their desired action onboard. John and I inserted all the MCC-H callouts and commands into the Software Integration Test procedure produced at KSC.

My other task was the more exciting of the two because of its locations on-console in the SSR for each mission. In short, I was part of the MCC-H mission operation as a first-time flight controller! I had reached the center of the universe as far as I was concerned. The tasks dealt with command histories and provided operations support to the Assistant Flight Director and Operations & Procedure positions in the front room. The team in the SSR also supported the Flight Director position in the front room.

I had that confirmed to me personally years later in a conversation with a nice lady who was married to Walt Cunningham at the time of the flight. Walt was part of Wally Schirra's astronaut crew for Apollo 7.

The Apollo 7 crew.

Her name was Lo Cunningham, long since divorced from Walt. I was lucky enough to have a date with her in (approximately) 1996. I believe the event was one of the many Apollo reunions held yearly in Houston, usually on the anniversary of the first Moon landing on July 20, 1969.

In a conversation with Lo about astronaut assignment and the politics involved, she expressed a concern that Walt had developed over the many years of the planning for the program that followed Apollo. It was eventually named Skylab and used the Apollo leftover hardware to establish the United States' first manned space station during the years 1973–1975.

During those years before launch, Walt worked long hours on the Skylab crew area's design and the astronaut procedures required to run the lab and all its experiments. Walt's dedication was motivated by the chance to be named one of the astronauts to fly aboard Skylab. He was never named. He expressed much of his disappointment to his wife, Lo. When she mentioned that neither of them knew why Walt was never assigned to any of the three three-man crews that flew to Skylab,

I popped up with, "I know why." Then I explained the Apollo 7 events back in 1967.

"But that was Wally's problem with the ground team headed by Chris," Lo tried to explain.

I did my best to gently explain Chris's mood and the rising reputation and power he had at the time. "Chris would not let him, because he was a member of the Apollo 7 crew!" My thought at the time was that Wally should have known when he left NASA that his career would forever be tied to Apollo 7 in the mind of Chris Kraft. The same was true for the other Apollo 7 crewmember, Don Eisele. No member of the Apollo 7 crew ever flew in space again.

Lo found it hard to believe until she spoke with one of her longtime friends, Mrs. Christopher Kraft. Mrs. Kraft, I was told later, explained the politics of "us boys" as best as she could to Lo Cunningham at the time.

Part 5: INCO in the MOCR

After serving in the back room SSR for most of Gemini (8–12) and early Apollo missions, I was promoted to the front room (MOCR) in a new position. As INCO, I was really at the center of the universe now! The position combined the communication systems responsibility for both the Apollo CSM and the LM lander. Responsibility included operation of all antennas, recorders, TV, and transmitters and receivers onboard. Voice circuits were also included. Maximizing signal strength for maintaining high-bit-rate telemetry was the primary task, so that all other flight controllers received the maximum data available from their respective systems. I remained in this front room position for all the Apollo missions to the Moon starting with Apollo 12. I also supported the Skylab Program as INCO. Skylab was the first space station built using Apollo hardware. The laboratory with its Apollo telescope mount was launched unmanned using the giant Saturn V moon rocket. The lab was outfitted using the Saturn third-stage S-IVB rocket body. Then other launches using the smaller Apollo rocket, the S-IB, delivered the three three-man crews to Skylab using the Apollo spacecraft CSM. The three crews manned Skylab over a period of nine months. Years later, long after Skylab missions were completed, the CSM reentered the atmosphere and parts of the mostly burned-up lab landed in Australia.

Apollo–Soyuz was our first mission with the Soviets, and the first international docking of two manned spacecraft. The three-man Apollo docked with the two-man Soyuz using a docking adapter built in the United States. Each spacecraft was launched (Soviets first) from their respective launch pads. Apollo was launched from Pad 39 at KSC and Soyuz was launched from what is now the Baikonur Cosmodrome in Kazakhstan. It was all the Soviet Union back in 1975 at launch.

On Apollo–Soyuz I reached my highest position of authority in mission control. Pete Frank was the lead Flight Director and he asked me to assist him at the Flight Director console. Pete told me that he was working hard to stay coordinated with the team in Mission Control Moscow. Many coordination calls from Moscow kept Pete a little too busy. He asked me to join him and answer all the calls to the Houston Flight Director in all the TCPs from all the test conductors of launch teams at KSC. I agreed to help.

These calls numbered many, especially in the last portion of the countdown before Apollo launch. Therefore, for the launch countdown and the launch phase, Pete and I were a team handling all the Flight Director duties from all locations. I supported Pete as assistant flight director with all the KSC prelaunch support calls. I handled all calls and performed all coordination required from the launch vehicle test conductor, the spacecraft test conductor, and the combined vehicle test supervisor. Pete selected me because I was well known to KSC personnel from my support to the ATIWG, and I had performed all the calls and actions required for coordination between the launch teams at KSC and the flight team in MCC-H. In short, I was a successful assistant flight director sitting next to Pete at the Flight Director console in Mission Control.

As a bonus for the tedious task of putting together all the TCPs with the KSC people, I was asked to perform as Flight Director during the prelaunch countdown for the Apollo–Soyuz Test Project (ASTP). See

Figure 17 below of me at the Flight Director console between Pete Frank and Don Puddy, the official Flight Directors for the mission.

Pete requested that I help him during the prelaunch. Normally during Apollo and Skylab missions the Flight Director assembles his team and provides all the support calls to KSC per the countdown TCP.

There were other times when either John Temple or I performed at the Flight Director console, but those were during early prelaunch tests when the entire Mission Control team was not required to support. Then John or I alerted the appropriate flight controller when he had to perform some step in the KSC procedure, such as sending a command from Houston. Those pad tests were usually minor tests where the Flight Director had a more important meeting or mission preparation task to attend that had priority over the pad test. John or I were the best ones to conduct the test, since we had helped write it at KSC and also distributed all the books to the right flight controllers in Houston.

When Pete asked, I had only one (stupid) condition. I was glad to help because I knew why he was asking for the ASTP mission. Pete was going to be even busier than normal because of demands on his time for coordination with the Soviet Flight Director in Moscow Mission Control, which involved translators in all status calls. I knew the Russian Flight Director, as John and I had worked with him when he was in Houston coordinating the simultaneous American and Soviet countdowns procedures. His name was Victor Blagov, and he certainly knew English better than we knew Russian! But the official language in each place was the native tongue. This complication put an extra burden on Pete in the launch countdown, where he could use some help to answer questions and perform all the countdown tasks required from KSC coming up to launch.

The other Flight Directors did not want to do that task for two reasons. First, they had their own shifts to prepare for on the mission and did not like the launch shift with all the KSC calls. Second, the Flight Directors were not as familiar with all the KSC calls in the countdown as were John and I. We knew all the key launch controllers and had worked with them in the countdown development. As a matter of fact, I think they were more comfortable talking to John and me for the Houston Flight Director calls, because we knew a little more about the KSC operations than our own Houston Flight Directors. This was to be expected, since we helped develop the TCP for the countdown and in most cases had conducted some of the early pad test from the Flight Director console.

The key prelaunch operation directors who made most of the calls to Houston Mission Control were the Spacecraft Test Conductor, Skip Chauvin; the Saturn Launch Vehicle Test Conductor, Chuck Henschel; and the Combined Vehicle Test Supervisor, Bill Schick.

Other isolated calls were made from the Launch Director to report milestone "Go," and from the Range Safety Officer for the Cape Canaveral tracking range sites and the Merritt Island Launch Annex Ground Station and Tracking Data Network, for launch tracking and telemetry forwarded to MCC-H. The only person of these three to join us at KSC for all the TCP development activity was George Jenkins from Merritt Island.

What was the stupid request of mine? Well, I guess it was not so stupid. But during the final countdown, the available space around the Flight Director console (the center of the universe!) was usually taken up by backup astronauts, the next shift Flight Director (Don), NASA headquarters management, or Chris Kraft. In other words, I would not have any spare space to plug in and handle all the KSC countdown calls. Pete understood my concern and promised that he would "save me a seat" in order to help him out while he was busy with the Russians.

I really enjoyed the status of Prelaunch Flight Director, the title I gave myself. And when I made the required calls, Skip, Bill, and Chuck all recognized my voice and gave me a special greeting on the loop that I shall never forget.

The ASTP launch was a special day for me. Then I was rewarded with my picture in the best aerospace magazine at the time, *Aviation Week*. (See Figure 17.) As you can see, I was sitting right between Pete and Don!

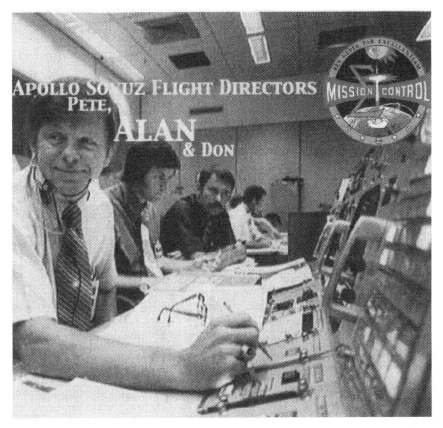

Alan at the ASTP Flight Director console.

Even Captain Kirk might have been a little jealous!

After the successful move *Apollo 13*, Tom Hanks began a TV project entitled *From the Earth to the Moon*.

As an owner of a Corvette bought the year we landed on the moon, I took a lot of kidding from the Apollo astronauts. You see, all the Moon-walking Apollo crews were given free Corvettes by General Motors. But, because I had to pay for mine, I had to put up with a lot of chaff from the guys who got free ones.

I enjoyed a little payback when *Corvette News* magazine was willing to publish two articles that I put together capturing how I used the car to get around Houston between all the busy appointments of "my seven lives." I titled one of the articles "I Lead Seven Lives."

Corvette News article lead.

One day I got a call from a person in Hollywood on Tom Hanks's staff. From much feedback on *Apollo 13*, it became clear that the movie folks had made an error with the Corvette that Tom drove in the movie. The Apollo 13 mission was launched in 1970; in the movie, they used a 1972 Corvette. The staffer couldn't see any difference in the cars. Of course, any Corvette owner knows the model differences down to the tiniest detail.

I ended up explaining Corvette minutiae over the phone to the staffer. And to make a long story short, the TV series that Tom put together was very successful. One reason, no doubt, was that all the Corvette owners who complained about *Apollo 13* were now satisfied because they used the correct year Corvette in the TV program.

My 1969 Corvette was a good car for me. I put over five hundred thousand miles on two engines and restored it for sale in 2009 after forty years of fun and ownership.

You're welcome, Mr. Hanks!

My familiarity with the KSC prelaunch tests began long before the fire with an early assignment from Gene Kranz, my branch chief at the time. This primary task became available to both John and me during the early Apollo planning timeframe, not long after the Gemini Program ended.

The Apollo pad tests and launch countdown at the Cape were getting more complicated, as was the Houston role during these major KSC tests. John Temple and I were assigned to represent the Houston teams at the newly formed ATIWG. This group met biweekly and John and I attended. Conference phone call participation was not considered appropriate for the face-to-face work that was accomplished at the ATIWG. John and I as single men fit right in with the heavy travel requirements.

Besides the four-volume Launch Countdown, Houston (as we were known) participated in approximately four other major pad tests. John and I were responsible for the details of that participation. Then we got an extra bonus that I loved but he did not seem to covet.

The length of the tests covered many days, and MCC-H participation was usually very short after long waits. The Flight Directors soon tired of the wasted time on their part, so they handed over the Houston Flight Director task during the tests to us! I could hardly believe it! Even though the spacecraft were not flying, I, Alan Glines, was asked to move over to *the* Flight Director console in *the* Mission Control Center and conduct the tests to their completion.

I tried not to get too excited about this new challenge. But I failed. I was truly drunk with power at the center of the center of the universe! I knew what I was doing because John and I had written the procedures in the ATIWG. The other controllers, at times, were lucky to even find their participation in the multivolume procedures. I always knew where our commands and callouts were in every test and every book. That I was not going to forget.

John and I were kept busy with this task and travel every two weeks, inserting the many technical details of the Houston participation into the TCPs of the major pad tests, including the four-volume TCP of Launch

Countdown. The launch team handed over mission responsibility to the Houston team when the launch vehicle cleared the forty-story (on Saturn V) umbilical tower. "Tower clear," it was called by the overall test supervisor at KSC. Then Houston Mission Control was in charge until splashdown at the end of the mission.

I gained another benefit from my prelaunch pad test flight assignments to make all these big books for the KSC tests correct. The incident, which seemed small at the time, probably had a greater impact on my family than anything I ever did.

Why? Because I am sure they believed that I was making a small contribution to the Apollo Program. But they were realistic, too. They knew that I was a very new and young person recently graduated from a well-respected but somewhat average university, so they were proud of me but surely assumed that my tasks and contribution to the total Apollo Program had to be in the category of modest. I was just too young and inexperienced for anything critical. What a shock they received during their first tour of the new Johnson Space Center!

My family was visiting for the first time during one of the Apollo prelaunch tests in 1968. The total KSC test was interlaced with Houston callouts, all of which John and I had inserted during our work in the ATIWG. Even though the Houston team did not have the primary responsibility for the spacecraft during the prelaunch timeframe, we participated nonetheless. And John and I made sure all the Houston callouts were inserted into the KSC procedure at the correct time. Additionally, we were responsible for making the Houston part of the total test schedule. The schedule for Houston required the correct controller for the system under test to be in the MCC prepared to perform that part of the test. Each test also required a Flight Director to be present to conduct the Houston part of the test in conjunction with the KSC action. The total test when the spacecraft was involved was conducted by the CSM Test Conductor at KSC. This man was usually Skip Chauvin, an extremely well qualified man familiar with all the CSM systems.

His call sign was MSTC for Master Spacecraft Test Conductor. John and I worked closely with Skip to assure that both teams came together with the correct procedure at the correct time for all the prelaunch tests. The test was Launch Countdown, at the end of which the Apollo total vehicle was launched. But many tests preceded this final count.

It was during one of these tests when my family members from Independence and Tulsa—my father, Clair Glines, Aunt Wilma, Uncle Ben, and Aunt Joy—came for a visit. I had arranged a tour of MCC-H for them, including access to the VIP viewing room just behind the MOCR in MCC-H so they could view the action they were used to seeing on TV. I wanted to show them my position there for upcoming missions. I was explaining the operation in progress and all the console positions that we saw through the soundproof glass. The control room was about half full of controllers with a Flight Director, which was normal for a pad test in support of a KSC prelaunch test. One of the new Flight Directors, Don Puddy, was directing the Houston team for the test. They were following the procedure that John and I had put together with Skip Chauvin and his team at KSC.

MOCR view from the VIP room.

I had just finished explaining all the MOCR positions to my family when I saw two controllers turned around and point at me. We could hear the Flight Director's comm channel in the VIP room but nothing was being said. Then Don turned around and looked where the controllers were pointing. To my shock, he raised his hand and signaled for me to leave the VIP room and come to his console. Turns out he just had a question for me on the test procedure. But picture this in the minds of my family: Young Alan, who was explaining the center of the universe, was just called to the Flight Director's console because they needed *him*! It might as well have been Captain Kirk calling me to his *Enterprise* control chair to help battle the Klingons!

I excused myself to my family and said I would be right back.

Ironically, Don was very apologetic for interrupting my tour with my family. I chuckled and assured him no apology was necessary. His calling me to the Flight Director's console right in the middle of an Apollo operation was tantamount to raising my family's impression of me to astronomical heights (pardon the pun). I was at the center of the universe, which was the highest possible pinnacle of pride for my family. I realized this and took my time answering Don's question. To this day I cannot remember his question; something about the TCP callout coming up next, I think.

When I returned to the VIP room to continue my explanations, the family wanted to know first what the team needed from me. I was honest and explained the question I'd been asked and why I was the expert to answer it. From that point, they hung on my every word and were never able to express their impression of Alan Glines, Master of the Center of the Universe!

As for me, for the rest of the day I don't think my feet ever touched the ground. Wow!

My family, including my dad, was already impressed with my job working in the main control room—on TV, no less! But nothing could have impressed them more than Don calling me in for a consultation on that day.

The family did not say much to me about the event. However, I heard much later that word got back to Tulsa and Independence, something to the effect that NASA cannot run that place called Apollo Mission Control without Alan Glines! One or two articles also appeared in the *Independence Reporter* to that effect. My family members there never forgot the event for the rest of their lives. The event became an oft-repeated story about me and my value to the Mission Control team at that time.

Part 6: A Guest INCO

The INCO position in Mission Control was probably one of busier positions in terms of sending commands to the CSM spacecraft. For example, on the two-day trip to the Moon known as Trans-Lunar Coast, the CSM was put into a slow, twenty-minute roll to evenly distribute the Sun's heat across the surface. Every ten minutes, the INCO transmitted commands to the spacecraft to switch the onboard antenna between omni B and omni D, to ensure a continuous flow of telemetry from the CSM for the flight controllers to constantly monitor all their onboard systems and subsystems, This operation was called Passive Thermal Control or PTC.

As the CSM approached the Moon, lunar distance required switching between high-bit-rate telemetry to low-bit-rate telemetry. This operation provided the communications margin in low-bit-rate to effect the switch through the disappearing omni antenna to the soon-to-appear omni on the other side of the spacecraft.

Once the spacecraft was in a safe orbit around the Moon, we in Mission Control wanted all the telemetry data that we could get. When the CSM was on the front side of the Moon, that data was transmitted in real-time through the large 85-foot deep-space dishes of the NASA Deep Space Network. However, in orbit the spacecraft was not always in view of the Earth. For a full orbit of the Moon, part of the orbit was on the backside of the Moon. The INCO still got that data for the team in MCC by using more commands to the onboard telemetry recorder in the CSM. It is only that from the backside of the Moon that data from the recorder was a little delayed.

The recorder was an actual tape recorder that needed to be rewound and switched from Record to Playback each orbit. The INCO was the controller in charge of recorder operation. Routine spacecraft operations, like those of the antennas and the recorder, were designed to not require the astronauts' attention. Instead, routine communication tasks were handled by the INCO using digital commands transmitted from the INCO console through the NASA ground network to the appropriate Deep Space Network site in view of the Moon and spacecraft.

During the Apollo 17 mission, on a night shift when the flight crew was asleep, I gained a ride to my shift by exchanging a unique opportunity with a neighbor friend of mine, Reda Martin. We both lived at Parkgate Apartments in Houston during this period.

The opportunity consisted of providing a temporary NASA badge for her entry into the MOCR. The CSM for Apollo 17 was just appearing from around the Moon on one of its orbits when Reda arrived at the INCO console. I sat her down at the INCO position and pointed out which commands to transmit (buttons to press) to stop and rewind the recorder. Thus Reda became the first female to transmit a command to the Apollo spacecraft at the Moon. For her record as proof, we provided Reda with a command history and marked the command that she sent. Many times when she has shared that story with friends, family, and acquaintances, people haven't believed her. At the time of Apollo 17, there were no lady flight controllers on any team in Mission Control. So Reda quietly gained a dubious title of the first lady to transmit a command to the Apollo at the moon.

Even though there have been many skeptics in her life, she knows the special place she retains with her command history proof and her friendship with one of the INCOs: yours truly! Reda was our first guest lady INCO during Apollo!

Reda's the good-looking one on my Corvette!

Part 7: On the *Enterprise* Runway

My last position with NASA found me supporting the shuttle astronauts out on the runway at Edwards Air Force Base. These runways were used to test the landing capability of the *Enterprise* because they had miles of desert overrun for any contingency.

The *Enterprise* went through a series of flight tests on its 747 carrier aircraft that included captive inert flights, with *Enterprise* unmanned; captive active manned flights; and free lights, manned for landing. These flights made up the Approach and Landing Test (ALT) Program intended to ready the space shuttle landings for later space missions.

In the first series of flights, the *Enterprise* was not manned or powered up. These were for the 747 pilots to get familiar with the orbiter *Enterprise* atop the 747 carrier aircraft. The second series saw the

Enterprise manned and powered with communications and telemetry transmitted to MCC-H. These flights allowed the astronauts to become familiar with the *Enterprise* while still attached to the 747 carrier aircraft. The third and final tests were manned, powered with the *Enterprise* releases from atop the 747 and piloted to a desert runway landing. Two astronaut crews performed multiple free flights. Crew No. 1 was Fred Haise from Apollo 13 and Gordon Fullerton, a rookie. Crew No. 2 was astronauts Joe Engle and Dick Truly. Joe was from Kansas and eventually flew multiple shuttle flights to space. Dick also piloted the shuttle to space and later rose to become the lead administrator of NASA in Washington, D.C.

One of my last assignments for NASA introduced me to southern California. The first shuttle was manufactured at a facility in Palmdale, CA, by Rockwell, which was also the prime contractor for the Apollo mother ship, the CSM. This assignment broke me out of Mission Control and teamed me up with the astronaut crews who had been assigned to fly the first shuttle orbiter.

Me on the left from astronauts Fred and Gordon.

The first space shuttle was not designed for orbiting in space, as it was somewhat of a model itself designed just for the landing tests on Earth. The shuttle concept was much different from Apollo, in that it was a combination vehicle that performed all the functions of a space machine: an integrated launch vehicle, a spacecraft for orbital flights only, and a delta-winged aircraft for returning from space for a runway landing on earth.

NASA created a complete flight program just to verify its new landing capability. The program was called ALT for Approach and Landing Test, all of which were to be performed right in Chuck Yeager's backyard.

Now, Chuck was unimpressed with the entire astronaut corps and the idea of spaceflight. Why? Because the pilot did not have the role that Yeager performed so well when he became the first man to break the sound barrier.

As a matter of fact, my job would probably not exist if it weren't for the orbital velocity that begged for assistance from the ground. (Chris Kraft explains this in his book better than I ever could, because he is the person who came up with the reason for Mission Control assisting the space pilot in his vehicle traveling at five miles per second.) Chuck broke the sound barrier on his own at over 712 mph in the high desert of California—the same place NASA planned to land the shuttle during ALT.

Why? Because southern California has the best weather and most forgiving runways on Earth. The 10,000-foot concrete runways are backed up by *seven miles* of overrun. A pilot can make a lot of landing mistakes in seven miles and still live to tell about it.

For just this reason, the shuttle (finally) provided a real flying machine that Chuck Yeager could respect. He showed it respect by arriving to congratulate our first ALT crew on their first landing at Edwards. I was on duty for that flight when Fred Haise and Gordon Fullerton first landed the *Enterprise* in 1977. Yes, the first orbiter was named after the starship of *Star Trek* fame. NASA failed to tell the public that the first one had not been destined for space, a point of frustration especially for all the "Trekkies." Therefore, the *Enterprise* did not attain very high velocities. The later orbiters that reached space traveled at about Mach 25, or 17,500 mph. Certainly faster than a speeding bullet!—but nowhere near warp 9 of the starship in my imagination.

As I recall, for the postflight debriefing there was a slightly larger crowd around General Yeager than there was around Fred and Gordon. For some reason, all pilots seem to know all pilots. And, of course, everyone at Edwards Air Force Base knew who Chuck Yeager was. Even me.

All free-flight landings by both crews of the *Enterprise* during ALT were successful. They paved the way to space shuttle flights in space, which was next on the schedule.

CHAPTER 7

California for Private Industry

Part 1: Handover to Palos Verdes Apartments

The ALT Program was my last set of missions for NASA as part of the Vehicle Integration Test Team (VITT). Through my trips to California runways, I became familiar with southern California, even taking a vacation or two in the area. Vacations also included a fantastic one to Pebble Beach. I liked what I saw in California and I was a little disappointed in the space program direction, going to Earth orbit only. That was not exploration comparable to Apollo, and Earth orbit was not exploration. Captain Kirk would agree!

I was already familiar with the space shuttle from ALT and eventually taught a course about it at TRW. But that was in the future. Back then, I decided to check out the job scene in private industry in the Los Angeles area.

I responded to a few job advertisements in the South Bay beach area of the city. I was attracted to TRW for two reasons: TRW's reputation in the space industry was excellent (they designed the Lunar Module Descent engine for the moon landings); and the company was located in the attractive Space Park area in Redondo Beach.

My success in landing the TRW job of my choice was immediate. An attractive offer was presented to me, and I accepted. I was hired as a Senior Mission Systems engineer. The offer included a significant increase in pay over my government salary. The next step was to resign from NASA. Most of my NASA colleagues could not understand why I was leaving my good position. When I explained my disappointment about no exploration in NASA's future, they still did not understand. I had a great NASA job. They were right about the job, but not about the future. And I was excited about the new opportunities in California.

My next big question was where to live. During the ALT flights, I had met one of the lady astronaut candidates, Anna Fisher. She was a guest of our director, George Abbey. When she learned that I was moving to her neighborhood in Los Angeles, she recommended an apartment complex where she lived with her husband, Bill. Bill also became an astronaut candidate. Of course, her selection as one of the first female astronauts meant that she would be moving to Houston. I visited the apartments in Palos Verdes overlooking the Pacific. They were beautiful, framed by a golf course also overlooking the Pacific. I was lucky enough to find a fabulous-view apartment available and immediately took it. Later I learned that the recommendation from Anna Fisher had carried a lot of weight with the manager.

This was my first ocean view apartment, and I was practically speechless from its beauty. This Kansas hayseed had come a long way. The drive to TRW was a little long in Hawthorne Boulevard traffic, but both my cars were trusty. My favorite car was a 1969 Corvette Stingray that I bought new during the year we landed on the Moon. It had a lot of Houston miles on it and was the subject of two *Corvette News* articles already. I drove my Datsun 200SX also, but it was not as much fun as the Corvette. Even my cars had an ocean view from their garage.

Part 2: TRW to Shuttle Teacher

Not long after joining TRW, I learned of an after-hours program at TRW. With my space shuttle background and the fact that TRW major payloads were scheduled for shuttle launch, I developed an idea for a course that I could teach and titled it "Space Shuttle Payload Integration." I proposed the course to the education department and it was accepted. Using my shuttle knowledge, pictures, and contacts in Houston, I prepared a hundred-page handout. This handout became very popular with all my students because of all the shuttle pictures and diagrams. Many managers wanted a copy for their desk. My course developed a waiting list of TRW employees anxious to learn about the shuttle for their payload work at the company. The course was conducted for several years.

Next up for NASA were the contracts for its new International Space Station. As a contributor to TRW's Space Station contracts, I was able to funnel the information into another course, "Space Station On-Orbit Assembly and Operations." It as popular as my shuttle course and included all the latest designs from NASA and its contractors. TRW was a bidder on and won several Space Station contracts. I worked most of them while teaching my new course. One Request for Proposals (RFP) from NASA called for management of the entire station. The work for the RFP in TRW was based in Reston, Virginia. Based on my NASA background, I was asked to work on this RFP and was transferred to Reston for the year it took to complete. This project developed some valuable new technical writing skills that I would use frequently in the future on many TRW proposals. However, TRW lost that particular contract.

Part 3: USC Master's to Adjunct Professor at USC

A benefit from our Air Force customer neighbor in LA was a University of Southern California (USC) Master's program taught locally for the younger Air Force officers in need of project management savvy. The university complied by offering a Master of Science in Systems Management, a high-tech MBA program. As it was also available to contractors, I jumped at the opportunity. Because I was a little older than my Air Force classmates, I became a bit of a student pest. I always had too many questions. One part-time professor claimed he planned to get even. He did. After graduation, I was offered such a part-time position as adjunct professor teaching in the same program, dealing with jerks just like me!

But I enjoyed the teaching experience. The course content was the same as I had just finished to get my master's degree. It was a good experience overall, except for the exams. I must confess that my exams were a lot of work and somewhat difficult for the students to comprehend. I later heard that my true and false questions were dreaded by the students. The problem was that I asked why a statement was false if it were false.

I would have taught longer if my assigned classes stayed in the South Beach area, but some were moved as far away as Lancaster. The driving distance was prohibitive.

CHAPTER 8

Europe, My New Home

Part 1: NASA is One Nation, but ESA is Fourteen!

(The current number of nations represented is larger.)

Not long after I settled into my new home in Hermosa Beach, California, complete with ocean views from the balcony above my new Jacuzzi, I got a call from Europe. Earlier I had moved from my Palos Verses apartment to owning my first home in Hermosa Beach. My friend and colleague from Mission Control at NASA contacted me. Mel Brooks was his name, and Mel was formerly a branch chief in FCD for the LM systems people when I left NASA in 1979. Mel left NASA about the same time. He had established a good consulting contract with the ESA people in Europe through a small company in Houston. Mel had the only European division of the company, called Hernandez Engineering. Mel was fluent in German and had many friends in ESA at the time. His contracts were expanding and he needed some NASA-oriented help from me in Europe.

At the time I was living in my first home in Hermosa Beach and doing fine at TRW on some Space Station and other contracts. I was working on some classified space shuttle missions at the time. So I had no good reason to leave TRW and California. However, the foreign opportunity in my field was impressive, and Mel sounded like he really needed my help. The offer was also attractive and included German lessons. My first location would Darmstadt, West Germany, at the ESA facility there called the European Space Operations Center. Their work closely paralleled Mel's and my experience with NASA.

After thinking about such a move and mulling over the salary increase, including business trips to Paris, Tuscany, Bordeaux, Matterhorn, and San Tropez, I decided to go for it. The fact that English was the required language at all the space centers was a big factor in my decision, as I was not fluent in any other language.

I got along well with my ESA counterparts and took a lot of teasing because I was an American. I remember hearing one joke many times. It was the one about a trilingual person speaking three languages, a bilingual person speaking two languages and what do you call a person who speaks one language? An American, of course!

The work turned out to be satisfying and useful to ESA. This Kansan really enjoyed the experience of another culture. I was really coming into my own as an international space consultant.

Part 2: Life in Europe: Germany's Autobahn to the Dutch Tulip Coast

After approximately three years in Darmstadt, our contract work moved to Holland. The ESA facility in Noordwijk was called the European Space Research and Technology Center, ESTEC for short. Its work was more oriented toward the spacecraft of Europe and ESA's part of the International Space Station, the Columbus Laboratory. This contract work was more closely associated with our NASA experience in Houston with manned spacecraft.

My seven to eight years in Europe were divided between local living near two space centers. The first was Seeheim-Jugenheim near the ESA European Space Operations Center in Darmstadt, West Germany; the second was Noordwijk, Holland, near ESTEC. In both places I chose to live amongst the local population rather than available American enclaves. (Pretty brave for a Kansan!) The business and personal experience were priceless. I definitely was not in Kansas anymore! And those binoculars on my Dutch beach condo balcony were only for my tourist visitors. I hardly noticed the European topless beaches, of course. Our technical contribution to the ESA programs, such as the Columbus Lab, was valuable to our ESA customers in dealing with an arrogant NASA. When our contracts ran out, it was with reluctance that we all returned to the USA.

CHAPTER 9

Back to the USA

Part 1: STS-80—Wakeshield!

My return to the United States was initially marked by mission control work for three small companies: Muniz Engineering, Inc., for STS-80; Naknan Technical Services in the Philippines and Los Angeles; and Volt Engineering Services, for Hughes satellite control.

The work for Muniz Engineering was solely for the mission control support provided to the space shuttle mission STS-80. This contract put me back to work at my favorite place: a spacecraft control console. Only this time I was a contractor, not a NASA employee.

I had considerable space shuttle experience at the time, from NASA ALT and past teaching ventures at TRW. My position was in the Payload Operations Control Center (POCC) for the Wakeshield payload. The POCC was conveniently located near my home at the time in League City, Texas. And the mission preparation reacquainted me with an astronaut friend, Dr. Story Musgrave. Story was assigned to fly aboard STS-80 in much the same capacity as me on the ground in the POCC. He was the Payload Officer on board for Wakeshield deployment, and I was the Payload Officer in the Wakeshield POCC. Our jobs were slightly different owing to location, though we rehearsed the mission together a number of times, with me at my position in the POCC and

Story in the shuttle simulator at NASA Johnson Space Center. Story's main task onboard was deployment and retrieval of the Wakeshield payload. My task was to monitor and control the free-flyer mission of Wakeshield while separated from the space shuttle. Telemetry and command was our main tool in the POCC for the mission. In these coordinated rehearsal tasks, Story and I got to know each other a little better and became closer friends. This was Story's sixth and final mission as an astronaut. He continued with NASA for a time after the mission until the opportunities took him elsewhere.

I like to use Story as an example when people at my speaking engagements ask how best to prepare to become an astronaut. Maximum education is the key, I say. Go as far in school as you can in a technical or scientific field. Story has a total of three Ph.D.'s (one M.D.) and five master's degrees. He is a surgeon at his home hospital. I hasten to say that one doesn't need eight degrees, but Story's education is still a good example for astronaut candidates.

Wakeshield was a payload designed and sponsored by the University of Houston science department. Its purpose was experimental. It was intended to test-manufacture highly pure semiconductor material. This was done inside a small laboratory positioned in the wake of the payload's direction of flight. In this way, a high degree of purity was achieved being shielded in its wake. Hence the name Wakeshield. The mission was a success in its third mission onboard the shuttle flight STS-80. Story deployed Wakeshield and the POCC team assured that it reached its higher orbit for its test operations.

When the operation was complete and it was retrieved and positioned back in the shuttle payload bay area, Story used the remote manipulator system arm to grasp the payload and position it in its payload bay slot. It was then returned to earth by the shuttle and delivered to the University of Houston for assessment of the purity of the semiconductor material. The results were successful. However, the need for an expensive space facility to produce the material was not established. Sufficiently pure semiconductors were being manufactured right here on Earth for the many high-tech products that required them. The Wakeshield was a successful experiment, but it never flew in space again.

Story and I went our separate ways when the Wakeshield payload contract was complete, although we have stayed in touch over the years.

My next contract opportunity was out of Naknan Technical Services headquarters in Houston. Loral Corporation had launched a communications satellite called Mabuhay for the government of the Philippines. Naknan won a contract to help the launch team check it out on-orbit. Checkout was to be performed from the mission control center at Subic Bay, Philippines, site of the former U.S. Naval Base. I was assigned to report there for the contract tasks. At Subic Bay we were housed in the former U.S. Naval Bachelor Officer's Quarters that was converted into a nice hotel. The mission control center was also located on the former U.S. Naval Base grounds. Loral had assembled a capable and talented assortment of personnel for the checkout from several contractors.

The checkout of the Mabuhay satellite was completed within one week of everyone's arrival. The Mabuhay name is Filipino for a friendly greeting. But there was one big problem. The orbit of the satellite was determined to be incorrect by causing interference with a Japanese satellite close by in geosynchronous orbit. So the satellite had to be moved to a different orbit. In its new location it was necessary to repeat the checkout already performed. This meant that the contractors had to be there for several more weeks. In that time we all got to know the Filipino people better, ranging from the satellite people to many service people at the hotel. And it was a good relationship. They seemed to like Americans.

As expected, the final checkout was completed with no problems. We all returned to the USA with many new friends from the contractor team there. I still keep in touch with my good friend Richard Dutchik, from Melbourne, Florida. And the Mabuhay satellite continues to function today for the Philippines.

Part 2: Back to California

Upon our return to the United States, Naknan won more contracts for satellite mission control work. Only this time the work was located in the LA area for the Hughes Corporation satellites on-orbit. My latest work in California before rejoining TRW in Redondo Beach and moving back to that area was on a mission control console at Hughes Aircraft Corporation. Hughes mission control was located in El Segundo, California. The control tasks were focused on new and existing giant communications satellites that primarily provided commercial communications for Hughes's respective customers.

Those customers included several international governments. In some cases the satellites were experiencing system problems. Our Naknan operations team was contracted to assist the Hughes personnel in troubleshooting the satellites. Successful testing of these problem areas led to new missions of communications and, in some cases, new customers. From the twenty-four-hour console work a number of friendships arose with our talented Hughes colleagues. We worked well together in the operations testing during the troubleshooting. All satellite procedures were accomplished to create the alternate missions required. Most of the satellites were repaired sufficiently to accomplish their planned missions. For those satellites that were rejected by the customers, new customers were found. And the reduced capability was successfully sold to the new customers. Hughes was lucky with its business to have a large number of communications satellite customers available for alternate reduced missions.

The commercial communications services were the primary purpose of these satellites and the business of Hughes Aircraft Corp. Our Naknan company provided the complete round-the-clock operations support team for these services for on-orbit test and checkout.

Each time a new satellite was launched and positioned in its orbit, our team was charged with conducting the complete on-orbit test plan. Our small team worked with the Hughes engineers who documented the test procedures as a cohesive, coordinated operations team.

During the limited contract time, I was able to investigate opportunities with my former employer, TRW in Redondo Beach. But before then I decided to make a company move for financial reasons. The Hughes job stayed the same; only my company changed, to Volt Engineering Services. Other members of my operations team also decided to move to Volt. That work continued for Hughes mission control for approximately one more year, to 2001. Meanwhile, the NASA national space program was no closer to *2001: A Space Odyssey* as depicted in the movie. Space shuttles were still flying to Earth orbit, only working on the International Space Station (ISS).

During 2001, it became time for another move as the Hughes work was completed. I was fortunate enough to find a good open position with TRW in the System Engineering organization at Space Park. I joined them with much new international operations experience and put that experience to work on new TRW contracts for NASA and the U.S. Air Force.

Not long after I rejoined TRW, Northrop Grumman bought the company and TRW became Northrop Grumman Space Technology (NGST). My work continued on a mixture of satellite projects and proposals on a wide variety of NASA and Air Force projects, some classified.

Part 3: On to Mars!

A later highlight at NGST was a proposal team for the new NASA hardware for Mars! We teamed with Boeing and two other major companies for this proposal. The program was NASA's new exploration program for reaching out to the asteroids and eventually to Mars. It was called the Crew Exploration Vehicle (CEV), or *Orion* by name.

The *Orion* spacecraft design.

The proposal work was with three other companies and included the spacecraft design and the complete operations plan for Mars missions. The operations plan was my focus, owing to my extensive background in that area. I developed multiple Operations Concept (OPSCON) scenarios for the proposal. As well, I documented additional products for the proposal, including elements of the Modular Operations System Architecture; and outlined products for the complete On-Orbit Test Plan to be included with the proposal. The scope of this plan and the OPSCON scenarios covered the complete mission set to Mars. They were applicable to *Orion* missions to the International Space Station and eventually to an asteroid in the asteroid belt between Earth and Mars.

For my proposal efforts, I received a NGST Commendation. However, our team of Boeing and NGST with other companies did not win the contract for *Orion*. Lockheed, our competitor, won it and is working on *Orion* final design and missions to this day.

The *Orion* CEV.

My Northrop Grumman CEV Commendation.

This CEV named *Orion* with a six-person crew is destined for missions at the Space Station, asteroid base, and eventual journey to Mars. Even though NGST teamed with Boeing did not win the *Orion* contract, the company became immersed in the proposal series for the Moon/Mars lander called *Altair. Altair* will be the complex manned vehicle that will establish our first base on an asteroid and eventually Mars. My proposal role once again called on my Apollo LM experience to contribute key operations heritage.

During the years following the *Orion* loss, a number of projects required my experience and assistance. I developed operations products, such as requirements and assorted trade studies, for the following projects:

1. OPSCON Tool Study.
2. Tracking and Data Relay Satellite (TDRS-K) Version K.
3. Alternate Infrared Satellite System (AIRSS).
4. National Polar Orbiting Environmental Satellite System (NPOESS).

These projects were large program efforts for NGST. They were not nearly as exciting as the Apollo missions I worked on in the 1960s, but they were my assignments at the time so I tackled them with my usual vigor that was rewarded in most cases. My usual vigor included applying my Apollo and subsequent operations experience to develop the required Concept of Operations OPSCON scenarios and many derived requirements in the process. All these products were delivered to the customer either in the proposal required or at the specific program's milestone review briefings and documents.

The OPSCON Tool Study focused on a standard set of software and briefing tools associated with the development of the OPSCON required for any particular unmanned satellite project. These tasks were designed to standardize the process of concept development. The tools also included standard methods for the development of OPSCON scenarios and their derived requirements. The final set of requirements was a key product in the design and development of any satellite project. Those OPSCON products became part of the overall Operations

Plan on each satellite project or program. The Operations Plan was also presented at the contract or proposal milestone reviews with the respective customers.

The TDRS-K was NASA's upgraded new-technology version of the Tracking and Data Relay Satellite (TDRS) system already in orbit, for which TRW was the original contract award winner. And the company (NGST) was interested in winning this follow-on proposal for the TDRS system. All versions of the current TDRS system of satellites were in use by NASA on all space shuttle and Space Station missions. Additionally, unmanned satellites used the TDRS system to relay telemetry to Earth for such projects as the Hubble Space Telescope. In short, the TDRS system was always busy with telemetry data relay to Earth. The existing satellites are real workhorses. And the new K version proposed was being competed by NGST and other companies for the new upgraded system that included interplanetary relay of telemetry signals.

Also along the lines of communications, I helped perform detailed trade studies for NASA for the next generation of advanced communications systems. These trade studies addressed the need for long-distance X-band relay satellites for missions like that planned for the journey to Mars. Such advanced systems required significant upgrades to the support ground systems. Therefore the trade studies addressed the ground system upgrades required, also.

For the AIRSS, I led a small but highly skilled OPSCON in the development of three products. We:

1. Produced and presented quality mission architectures.
2. Developed a draft Concept of Operations (CONOPS) document.
3. Developed key OPSCON scenarios.

These products allowed the derivation of AIRSS system requirements to be presented at the major milestone System Requirements Review for the Air Force customer. The System Requirements Review featured the Concept of Operations in the context of detailed OPSCON scenarios covering all mission phases of the AIRSS satellites.

Many of the same products were developed for the NPOESS Program, only in this case the mission of the satellite constellation was focused on United States and world weather. Weather from the satellites included not only the current conditions over the world but enough data to generate highly accurate forecasts for all the USA and isolated war zones around the world. The OPSCON scenarios also dealt with satellite contingencies and backups and their recovery to obtain the required weather data. The NPOESS Program represented a major upgrade to the USA and the world weather monitoring and forecasting. Our company, Northrop Grumman, had won the NPOESS contract as a major program to design, build, and launch all the required satellites to cover the world from polar orbit.

Also developed were special innovative Intensive Calibration Validation procedures and test plan. This plan, coupled with the special OPSCON scenarios, produced an extra contract award fee from the customer, the National Oceanic and Atmospheric Administration. I was particularly proud of this accomplishment and its product value to the NPOESS program. It was a major contribution to the overall NPOESS Operations Plan.

Equally valuable to the company were all my operations-oriented contributions to the four programs and proposal.

Epilogue

Very early in life, I learned the value of a dollar. I could even reach the cliché of "penny pincher" at times during my early boyhood years. Not only was I somewhat of a nerd, but also I was cheap!

One of my first jobs, when I was about ten, was as a delivery boy. I was employed by the Halsey Dry Goods store to deliver packages to customers on my bike after school. I remember really looking forward to my first paycheck at my grand salary of $3 per week.

What a letdown for this penny pincher when I opened it and found $2.97! "Where's my missing three cents?!"

That three cents is not missing and is very important to you, I was told by my friend Mary at the cosmetics counter. It goes to a place called Social Security for your retirement years. My unspoken response at the time was something like, What in the world is a ten-year-old doing saving three cents for retirement?

But this early example of my penchant for thrift stayed with me over the years. It came in handy as our family, as any family, suffered some financial ups and downs.

Another financial milestone was preparing for college. I did my part with good efforts as a student. I remember my father saying that he had a good savings account for my college available as early as junior high. However, when it came time for me to access those funds, I was shocked to learn that they were long gone from helping our family survive some of those "downs."

It was time for me to go to Plan B, which consisted of me paying for college myself from my multiple scholarships, job wages, and a student loan.

Even to this day, I tend to keep a close watch on my funds. Surviving a year out of work strengthened that resolve even more. My friend Ron Vega, who is also my excellent barber, has found a nickname for me after he observed my acquisition of more than one imitation Rolex and the sale price on my 1969 Corvette that I purchased new for about $5,000 and recently refurbished to new condition with a price tag of $16,000.

But those were 1969 dollars, I keep telling Ron.

He still calls me Dr. Greed! "Greed is good!"

The "spaced out" nature of my adventures stretching from the Gemini Program through Apollo, to all my adventures in Europe and culminating with many projects in Northrop Grumman, attest to the varied experiences I've had all over the world. These confirm in my mind the international value to mankind of a continuing manned space program. The experience level is not just limited to the excitement of the Apollo main control room. That goal of mine from my early days of Star Trek was finally reached in my Mission Control tasks. This Kansas boy achieved his dream of some control of the universe stemming from his love of the starship Enterprise control console to my NASA INCO control console in Houston. And further dreams were realized as my work on space projects evolved. My goal stretched to Europe and the Philippines in the aerospace world of private industry before returning to the Los Angeles area for the culmination of a long but fulfilling career in aerospace. The overall value of the American space program was always apparent to me in all my tasks and travels, especially stemming from my personal experiences in Apollo Mission Control-Houston.

Glossary

AIRSS	Alternate Infrared Satellite System
ALT	Approach and Landing Test
ASTP	Apollo Soyuz Test Project
ATIWG	Apollo Test Integration Working Group
BSEE	Bachelor of Science in Electrical Engineering
CAPCOM	Capsule Communicator
CEV	Crew Exploration Vehicle
CLTC	Combined Launch Vehicle Test Conductor
CONOPS	Concept of Operations
CSM	Command Service Module
CVTS	Combined Vehicle Test Supervisor
DCS	Digital Command System
DJ	Disk Jockey
ESA	European Space Agency
ESOC	European Space Operations Center
ESTEC	European Space Research and Technology Center
FCC	Federal Communications Commission
FCD	NASA Flight Control Division
FCOD	Flight Crew Operations Directorate
FCOB	NASA Flight Control Operations Branch
FDSSR	Flight Director Staff Support Room
FORTRAN	Formula Translation computer language
FSD	NASA Flight Support Division
GSFC	NASA Goddard Spaceflight Center
ICC	Independence Community College

INCO	Integrated Communications Officer
ISS	International Space Station
JSC	NASA Johnson Space Center
KIND	Independence Kansas Radio Station call letters
KOMA	Oklahoma City Oklahoma Radio Station call letters
KSC	NASA Kennedy Space Center
KU	University of Kansas
LA	Los Angeles
LM	Apollo Lunar Module
MACH-2	Twice the speed of sound
MBA	Masters in Business Administration
MCC	Mission Control Center
MCC-H	NASA Mission Control Center-Houston
MCC-K	NASA Mission Control Center-Kennedy
MOCR	Mission Operations Control Room
MSC	NASA Manned Spacecraft Center
MSFN	Manned Spaceflight Network
MSOB	Manned Spacecraft Operations Building
MSTC	Master Spacecraft Test Conductor
NASA	National Aeronautics and Space Administration
NGST	Northrop Grumman Space Technology
NPOESS	National Polar Orbiting Environmental Satellite System
OCP	Operational Checkout Procedure
OPSCON	Operational Concept

PBI	Push Button Indicator
POCC	Payload Operational Control Center
PTC	Passive Thermal Control
RFP	Request For Proposal
S-V	NASA Apollo Saturn Five Lunar Launch Vehicle
S-IB Vehicle	NASA Apollo Saturn One-B Orbital Launch
S-IVB Stage	NASA Apollo Saturn Four-B Launch Vehicle
SSR	Mission Control Staff Support Room
TCPs	Test Checkout Procedures
TDRS	Tracking and Data Relay Satellite
TRW CA	Private aerospace company in Redondo Beach,
TTY	Teletype
TEX	Texas (Corpus Christi tracking site)
USB	Unified S-Band
VITT	Vehicle Integration Test Team